INSTANT VORTEX AIR FRYER COOKBOOK

Easy & Budget-Friendly Air Fryer Recipes

For Beginners & Advanced Users

BY
Audrey Coleman

ISBN: 978-1-952504-97-6

COPYRIGHT © 2020 BY Audrey Coleman

All rights reserved. This book is copyright protected and it's for personal use only. Without the prior written permission of the publisher, no part of this publication should be reproduced, distributed, or transmitted in any form or by any means, including photocopying, recording, or other electronic or mechanical methods.

This publication is sold with the idea that the publisher is not required to render accounting, officially permitted, or otherwise, qualified services. If advice is required, it is necessary to seek the services of a legal or professional, a practiced individual in the profession. This document is geared towards providing substantial and reliable information in regards to the topics covered.

DISCLAIMER

The information written in this book is for educational and entertainment purposes only. Strenuous efforts have been made to provide accurate, up to date and reliable complete information. The information in this book is true and complete to the best of our knowledge. All recommendations are made without guarantee on the part of the author and publisher.

Neither the publisher nor the author takes any responsibility for any possible consequences of reading or enjoying the recipes in this book. The author and publisher disclaim any liability in connection with the use of information contained in this book. Under no circumstance will any legal responsibility or blame be apportioned against the author or publisher for any reparation, damages, or monetary loss due to the information herein, either directly or indirectly.

Table of Contents

INTRODUCTION ... 6
Meaning of Instant Vortex Air Fryer ... 7
Benefits of Using the Instant Vortex Air Fryer ... 8
Instant Vortex Air Fryer Functions & Buttons ... 10
Steps to Ensure that Instant Vortex Air Fryer Works Properly ... 12
Instant Vortex Air Fryer Accessories Cleaning Method ... 14
Helpful Tips for Cooking with the Instant Vortex Air Fryer ... 15
Instant Vortex Air Fryer Troubleshooting ... 16
Instant Vortex Air Fryer Frequently Asked Questions & Answers ... 18
INSTANT VORTEX AIR FRYER BREAKFAST RECIPES ... 20
Zucchini Hash Browns ... 20
Valentine's Day Egg Casserole ... 21
Steel Cut Oatmeal ... 22
Spinach and Egg Casserole ... 23
Southwest Eggs ... 24
Shakshuka ... 25
Pumpkin Porridge ... 26
Quiche Boats ... 27
Omelet ... 28
Mini Egg Muffins ... 29
INSTANT VORTEX AIR FRYER LUNCH RECIPES ... 30
Fall off the Bone Ribs ... 30
Sweet Beet Chips ... 31
Whole-Wheat Pizzas ... 32
Curry Chickpeas ... 33
INSTANT VORTEX AIR FRYER POULTRY RECIPES ... 34
Mississippi Roast Chicken Style ... 34
Mayo Fresh Herb Chicken ... 35
Mayo Parmesan Chicken ... 36
McCormick Chicken Ole ... 37
Mediterranean Chicken ... 38
Lemon Greek Chicken ... 39
Lemon Orange Chicken Breast ... 40
Lemon Pepper Chicken ... 41
Moroccan Spiced Chicken Thighs ... 42

Japanese Style Chicken Curry	43
INSTANT VORTEX AIR FRYER BEEF & PORK RECIPES	44
Brisket	44
Braising Steaks	45
Bottom Round Roast	46
Roast Beef	47
Beef Wrapped Asparagus	48
Brown Gravy	49
Beef Tips in Mushroom Sauce	50
BBQ Ribs	51
Creamy Ranch Pork Chops	52
INSTANT VORTEX AIR FRYER FISH & SEAFOOD RECIPES	53
Tomato Tilapia	53
Shrimp with Mango Mango Preserves	54
Shrimp Teriyaki	55
Shrimp Scampi with Linguini	56
Boiled Shrimp	57
Shrimp Scampi with Zucchini	58
Shrimp Linguine Alfredo	59
Shrimp Scampi	60
INSTANT VORTEX AIR FRYER SOUP RECIPES	61
Super Quick Potato Soup	61
Sweet Potato and Black Bean Chili	62
Sweet Potato Chili	64
Sweet Potato Lentil Soup	65
Stuffed Pepper Soup	66
Spinach and Ravioli Soup	67
Split Pea Soup	68
Spaghetti Sauce with Meat	69
INSTANT VORTEX AIR FRYER RICE & PASTA RECIPES	70
Spanish Rice	70
Frito Enchilada Casserole	71
Frozen Stuffed Shells with Frozen Italian Sausage	72
Swedish Meatballs & Medium Shells with Alfredo Sauce	73
Sweet Potato Enchilada Casserole	74
Spinach Artichoke Pasta	75

Spinach Pesto Pasta..76

Spicy Sausage Pasta...77

INSTANT VORTEX AIR FRYER VEGETABLE RECIPES 78

Stuffed Peppers with Turkey...78

Stuffed Portobello Mushrooms..79

Stuffed Zucchini...80

Stuffed Zucchini Boats...81

Jimmy's Crack Slaw..82

Kale and Garlic..83

Ore-Ida Zesty Texas Cut Fries and Tater Tots..84

Pierogies...85

INSTANT VORTEX AIR FRYER APPETIZER RECIPES..86

Spinach Artichoke Dip...86

Totino's Frozen Party Pizza 87

White Castle Frozen Burgers..88

Queso 89

Teriyaki Chicken Wings...90

Sweet and Sour Meatballs...91

Tamale Dip...92

Spinach Artichoke Dip...93

Steak and Beef Nachos 94

Sticky Spicy Barbecue Wings..95

Steak and Beef Nachos 96

INSTANT VORTEX AIR FRYER DESSERT RECIPES 97

Grandmothers Pound Cake 97

Half a Cake 98

Funfetti Cupcakes...99

Duncan Hines Red Velvet Cake 100

Dump Cake-Apple Spice 101

Dump Cake-Fresh Blueberries... 102

Divine Boxed Brownies... 103

Corn Pudding... 104

Cranberry Banana Cake 105

Christmas Nut Clusters 106

Cinnamon Caramel Apples 107

INTRODUCTION

Modern ways of cooking are becoming more interesting as the Instant Vortex Air Fryer takes it to another level and expanded its line of countertop units. Instant Vortex Air Fryer is the latest cooking appliance and it has a capacity of cooking to cook about four meals at the same time. It should be noted that the Vortex Plus is not a toaster oven. This mean there's no toast setting.

The Instant Vortex Air Fryer doesn't belong in the Air Fryer ratings because it is more than an Air Fryer. The Instant Vortex Air Fryer has a mini convection oven with a maximum oven temperature of 400°F which has the capacity to air-fry, bake, roast, cook rotisserie style, broil, reheat, and dehydrate. The Instant Vortex Air Fryer is about $13"^2$ in size. Series of tests has been put through in other ascertain the durability and uniqueness of this unit and also to assess each of its functions which includes air-frying wings and fries, roasting whole chickens, baking cookies and muffins, reheating frozen lasagna, broiling burgers, and dehydrating fruit. It became perfect and successful.

Meaning of Instant Vortex Air Fryer

Instant Vortex Air Fryer is the latest cooking appliance and it has a capacity of cooking to cook about four meals at the same time. The Instant Vortex Air Fryer uses rapid air circulation to cook food, giving the good all the crispy rich flavor of deep frying under the usage of little or no oil.

However, air frying replaces hot oil with super-heated air in which the air is circulated in order to produce the same crunchy taste and texture that makes deep fried food so good. With the Instant Vortex Air Fryer, you can Air Fry, Roast, Bake, Broil, Reheat, Dehydrate and Rotisserie cook your food.

The Instant Vortex Air Fryer traps juicy moisture inside the crispy coating, but it does so without all the things that make people avoid deep frying: it's quicker, easier to clean, cooks healthy foods and the unit is easy to operate.

Benefits of Using the Instant Vortex Air Fryer

1. **The Instant Vortex Air Fryer is a 4-in-1 unit:**

This means that the Instant Vortex Air Fryer can perform four functions which include air-frying, roasting, baking, and reheating. The word Instant means that the unit can heat up fast, meaning you're ready to go in an instant.

2. **The Instant Vortex Air Fryer is compacted on size:**

The Instant Vortex Air Fryer looks so portable. The size is attractive because it doesn't occupy a lot of space in your counter. This means that the unit doesn't waste a lot of space on your counter but it still packing in 5.7Ls of air frying capacity. The Instant Vortex Air Fryer is big enough to fit a 2 Lbs. bag of fries or a 4 Lbs. chicken.

3. **The Instant Vortex Air Fryer cooks healthy foods:**

With the Instant Vortex Air Fryer, you can cook delicious and healthy even at a fastest speed. The Instant Vortex Air Fryer is easy to use thereby enabling you to use single-button Smart Programs and lock in flavor and nutrients without putting any harmful oils or fats to the food.

4. **Cooking with the Instant Vortex Air Fryer is very easy:**

This is true because the display unit of the Instant Vortex Air Fryer is not cumbersome to understand. You just need to set the working temperature and the cooking time and then you forget about the cooking process because the unit will do the rest of the cooking stuff within a short period of time.

5. **Instant Vortex Air Fryer controls are clear and simple to be understood:**

The control panel of the Instant Vortex Air Fryer was aesthetically designed to suit it outward appearance and also making it easier for the user who is a beginner to independently understand what is displayed on the control panel. The double displays on the Instant Vortex Air Fryer give accurate time and temperature readings, while 8 simple touch controls provide instant control over all cooking settings.

6. **Instant Vortex Air Fryer is easy to clean:**

Some people do feel reluctant to clean the kitchen appliance after use because it may be so tedious and sometimes take longer time to clean the appliance. The Instant Vortex Air Fryer is far above this fact. It is very easy to clean both the internal and external body parts. Most of the accessories are dishwasher safe. You just need to use a soapy water and do a proper cleaning after each use.

Instant Vortex Air Fryer Functions & Buttons

1. **Bake:**

This is another unique button that helps to cook for both the outside and the inside to be properly cooked. Some kitchen appliances can cook food and the outside turns brown but the inside still remain some raw ingredients not properly cooked. The bake button overcomes this. The Instant Vortex Air Fryer did a better job baking corn muffins, which were uniform in color and done both inside and outside.

2. **Roasting and rotisserie:**

If you are someone that likes roasted food like chicken then it is needless to go to grocery and get it because Instant Vortex Air Fryer is capable of roasting chicken according to your desired consistency. With the rotisserie spit, you can roast a chicken and it turn out tender and crispy brown in 50 minutes.

3. **Reheat:**

This button makes Instant Vortex Air Fryer to be unique. It helps to evenly heat up food after cooking for 15 minutes.

4. **Air-fry:**

The Instant Vortex Air Fryer makes wave here. This button is used to cook delicious food and make it crispy using one, two or three-quart cooking tray. This button aids in cooking food faster. For instance, frozen chicken nuggets can be properly cooked within 15 minutes. Frozen chicken wings took 30 minutes to bring to be properly cooked to your desired consistency.

5. **Broil:**

The Instant Vortex Air Fryer can bring a food to a broil. You just need to pop the food into Instant Vortex Air Fryer and hit the broil button; the result will be so perfect.

6. **Dehydrate:**

This button is perfect for those who are not in a haste to cook the food and serve within few minutes. Using the dehydrate button can slowly cook food for about 4 to 6 hours and it will still give the same result unlike other cooking modes.

7. **Time:**

This button is used to set the cooking cycle. It has a plus (+) or minus (-) sign I which you have to adjust the time by increasing it using the plus (+) sign and reducing it using the (-) minus sign.

8. Temperature:

This button is used to set the cooking temperature. You can adjust it using the + or - buttons.

7. Start:

This is used to commence the cooking process. When the ingredients have been placed in the unit, the next thing is to press the Start button to commence the cooking process. It is interesting.

8. Cancel:

This is used to cancel the entire cooking process. If there's any mistake somewhere, you can press the cancel button and everything will be cancelled.

Steps to Ensure that Instant Vortex Air Fryer Works Properly

1. **Open the Oven Door:**

The first thing to do is to place the drip pan on the bottom of the cooking chamber and then you close the oven door.

2. **Plug the Power Cord into the Power Source:**

Ensure that the power cable is firmly plugged in the power source. If the display reads "OFF" it shows that oven is in Standby mode.

3. **On the control panel, touch the Instant Vortex Air Fry Smart Program control:**

This will pop up a menu to set the cooking temperature. You should note that the default Air Fry Smart Program cooking temperature is 400°F.

4. **Touch the plus (+) or minus (-) in order to adjust the cooking time to your desired time:**

You should note that Smart Programs automatically save your previous time and temperature settings.

5. **Press Start:**

When you press this, the cooking process will commence following the cooking time and temperature settings. If you wants to adjust the cooking time and temperature, use the (+) or (-).

6. **When the Cooking Time is Completed, the Display Reads "Add Food":**

When this happen, do not add food to the cooking chamber because the food is properly cooked already.

7. **Open the Oven Door:**

You can use oven mitts and carefully place both cooking trays into the heated cooking chamber. Close the oven door while the cooking process commences. Note that the cooking time and temperature will be displayed.

8. **Part way Through the Cooking Time, the Oven Beeps and Displays "turn Food":**

This beep reminds you to turn your food. When you open the oven door, the cooking time will be automatically paused and begins when you close.

9. **For the Last Minute of Cooking Time, the Display Will be Counting the Last Minute of Cooking Time in Seconds:**

Immediately the cooking cycle is completed, display reads "End". Serve your food.

Instant Vortex Air Fryer Accessories Cleaning Method

Anytime you want to clean your Instant Vortex Air Fryer, ensure to unplug it from power source and allow it to cool off. Do not use harsh chemical detergents or scouring pads on any of parts.

- **Rotisserie Basket:**

For best results, you have to clean this part after every use. For best result, bristled brush is recommended instead of using a sponge. Sometimes you may spray with non-stick cooking spray before putting food.

- **Rotisserie Spit and Forks:**

Always remove this part and clean after each use.

- **Cooking Trays:**

When you are cooking, do not close the cooking tray to enable free air circulation. Always clean after every use. It is advisable not to use metal utensils when cleaning the cooking tray because it have a non-stick coating.

- **Rotisserie Lift:**

Always clean this part after each use.

- **Drip Pan:**

Disassemble and clean after every use. All food residue must be removed properly.

- **Cooking Chamber:**

Ensure to clean the cooking chamber walls after every use. Check the heating coil for food debris and properly clean the heating coil. Before the next use, ensure that the coil is dry completely. Ensure the heating coil is dry before next use.

Helpful Tips for Cooking with the Instant Vortex Air Fryer

1. If you are cooking pizza, put both cooking trays into the oven and place the pizza on the bottom cooking tray.
2. In order to prevent excess steam or splatter, always pat moist food items dry before cooking.
3. Apart from the rotisserie-cooked foods, most foods will benefit immensely from a preheated oven. You have to wait for the display to show "Add Food" before placing food in the cooking chamber.
4. If you want to cook any coated food items, always choose breadcrumb batters over liquid-based batters to enable the batter to stick to the food.
5. Flip the food over to the other side when the display shows "turn Food" for a proper cooking on both sides.
6. For golden fries, crispy, soak fresh potato sticks in ice water for about 15 minutes, you have to pat dry and lightly spray with cooking oil before putting them into the oven.
7. Ensure to use an oven safe baking dish and cover food with foil if you are baking cake, pie, quiche, or any food with filling or batter in order to prevent the top from overcooking or burning.
8. Make use of the drip pan when you are cooking fragile foods. Note that the drip pan doubles as a flat cooking tray.
9. In order to get the best and optimum result that you need, make use of the Smart Programs as a starting point and experiment with cooking times, and temperatures.
10. Before you press the start button on the display panel to begin the cooking process, ensure you place the rotisserie accessories and food in the oven.
11. In order to prevent excess smoke, always remove and empty the drip pan from time to time. You should note that air frying can cause oil and fat to drip from foods.
12. Always spray food items with cooking spray before applying seasoning to enable the seasoning adhere to food items.

Instant Vortex Air Fryer Troubleshooting

1. My Instant Vortex Air Fryer is Plugged in But it Does not Turn On:

Check and confirm that the power cord is firmly plugged in. Also examine the cord properly to check if the cord is faulty. If it is faulty, kindly replace it with new one. Do not manage any faulty cord to avoid electric shock.

2. I Found Food Residue on the Bottom of the Cooking Chamber:

To resolve this, press cancel on the display panel, unplug the oven and keep it to cool to room temperature. You also need to disassemble all accessories from the cooking chamber and ensure to clean all the area.

3. The Circuit or Heating Element is Faulty:

To resolve this, press cancel on the display panel, unplug the oven and keep it to cool to room temperature. Do not try to repair the appliance by yourself instead contact customer care.

4. White Smoke is Coming out From my Instant Vortex Air Fryer:

This could be caused by cooking food that are high in fat content like bacon, sausage, and hamburger. To resolve this, avoid foods with a high fat content. You also need to check drip pan for excess fat and remove as needed after cooking.

5. Water is Vaporizing Producing Thick Steam:

Always pat dry wet food ingredients before cooking. Note that you do not have to add water to cooking chamber when cooking.

6. Seasoning I Added to Food Has Blown into Element:

You have to be extremely careful when seasoning food. It is recommended that you spray your food before adding seasoning so they adhere to the ingredients.

7. Black Smoke is Coming From my Instant Vortex Air Fryer:

This could be caused by using oil with a low smoke point. To resolve this, press cancel on the display panel, unplug the oven and keep it to cool to room temperature. You also need to disassemble all accessories from the cooking chamber and clean the area.

Alternatively, you can use a neutral oil with a high smoke point, such as Virgin Olive Oil, Avocado, Canola, soybean or Safflower oil etc.

8. **My Instant Vortex Air Fryer is not Powered When Plugged:**

Use the same power cable and plug in another appliance to check if the fault is from the cord, circuit or the unit. This however can be as a result of oven door being open. The oven door was meant to be closed when you want to cook.

9. **The Display Pop Up Flash and A Code:**

If it shows E1, it means broken circuit of the thermal sensor. If it shows E2, it means short circuit of the thermal sensor. Contact customer care to resolve the two issues.

Instant Vortex Air Fryer Frequently Asked Questions & Answers

1. **What can I bake in the Instant Vortex Air Fryer?**

Any food that a conventional oven can bake, you can bake in the Instant Vortex Air Fryer. You just need to use any oven-safe baking dish that fits in the Instant Vortex Air Fryer.

2. **How does the Instant Vortex Air Fryer Works?**

This is a unique home appliance. It makes use of a powerful fan in order to circulate hot air around the food. The circulated hot air makes the food to quickly brown and give it a crispy, deep-fried flavor and texture without the deep frying. The maximum temperature of the Instant Vortex Air Fryer is 205°C or 400°F.

3. **What type of foods can I cook in the Instant Vortex Air Fryer?**

Absolutely all kinds of food can be cooked in this appliance. All your foods like sausage, schnitzel, steak, pizzas, pies, cakes, fries, wings and mozzarella sticks, kale, beet, and sweet potato chips, or homemade fruit leather roll-ups and so much more. The Instant Vortex Air Fryer is also a fast and convenient way to reheat leftovers.

4. **Is Cooking with the Instant Vortex Air Fryer Healthier than Deep Frying?**

The answer is Yes!!! Generally, Air-frying is a healthier option in food preparation. Deep frying will involve submerging food in oil or fat but air-frying will only require you to toss your food in a small amount of oil to give beautiful, crispy golden chicken wings, fish, mushroom caps, and much more.

5. **Are There Any Food That Cannot be Cooked with Instant Vortex Air Fryer?**

Any food that a conventional oven can possibly cooked can be cooked with the Instant Vortex Air Fryer. For optimum performance, it is advisable to cook place food in a single layer and cook in batches. You can equally avoid foods dipped in batter like calamari, tempura shrimp and buttermilk fried chicken.

6. **How Much Food can Contain in My Instant Vortex Air Fryer?**

For optimum performance, it is advisable to cook place food in a single layer and cook in batches. You don't need to crowd food items so that the food has enough space for hot air to circulate around the food.

7. **Do I Need to Preheat Instant Vortex Air Fryer Before Cooking?**

It is recommended to preheat the unit before cooking as most food items need high heat of a preheated cooking chamber. Preheating the unit can take up to 5 minutes.

8. **What Will Happen If I Don't Turn My Food When the Unit Pops Up" Turn Food" Option?**

The Instant Vortex Air Fryer was programmed to beep part way through the cooking time to remind you turn your food. If you don't turn your food when the unit beeps for that, the unit will continue cooking at the selected temperature until the cooking cycle is completed. In the other hand, if u doesn't turn your food when the unit beeps for that, it may result in uneven cooking.

9. **Can I Use My Instant Vortex Air Fryer to Crisp Frozen Fries and Fish Sticks?**

The answer is yes!!! The Instant Vortex Air Fryer is an easy way to add crispness to your favorite delicious meals.

10. **My food is Not Crispy. Is There Anywhere I am Doing Wrong?**

The Instant Vortex Air Fryer was programmed to make deep-fried results without being submerged in oil. You need to pat dry moist food items with a clean dish paper towel.

INSTANT VORTEX AIR FRYER BREAKFAST RECIPES

Zucchini Hash Browns

Preparation Time: 10 minutes

Cook Time: 10 minutes

Total Time: 20 minutes

Serves: 4

Calories: 285 kcal

Ingredients:

- 4 Medium zucchini, shredded
- 1 Tsp. salt
- ¼ Cup of flour
- 4 Eggs
- ½ Cup of shredded parmesan cheese
- ½ Tsp. pepper

Cooking Instructions:

1. Put salt into the shredded zucchini. Combine well and place in a strainer and set aside for about 10 minutes. Press to drain the water from the zucchini.
2. Combine together the flour, eggs, parmesan cheese and pepper. Make 4 patties. Place the mixture in the cooking trays with an even layer.
3. Lay the drip pan in the bottom of the cooking chamber. Select Air-fry on the display panel. Set the temperature to 370°F.
4. Adjust the cooking time to 10 minutes. Press the start. When the display panel show "Add Food", put the cooking tray in the center position.
5. When the unit show "turn food", ignore because the food is done.
6. Serve and enjoy!!!

Valentine's Day Egg Casserole

Preparation Time: 10 minutes

Cook Time: 20 minutes

Total Time: 30 minutes

Serves: 4

Calories: 307 kcal

Ingredients:

- 1 Can of Pillsbury biscuits
- 10 Eggs
- ½ Cup of milk
- Cooked bacon- sliced
- Cooked sausage, sliced into medallions
- Cheddar cheese

Cooking Instructions:

1. Cut the biscuits into four places. Layer in the cooking tray. Combine together the eggs and milk. Pour over the biscuits. Put the sausage, bacon and top with cheese.
2. Lay the drip pan in the bottom of the cooking chamber. Select Airfry on the display panel.
3. Set the temperature to 370°F and adjust the cooking time to 20 minutes.
4. Press the start. When the display panel show "Add Food", put the cooking tray in the center position.
5. When the unit show "turn food", ignore because the food is done.
6. Serve and enjoy!!!

Steel Cut Oatmeal

Preparation Time: 5 minutes

Cook Time: 13 minutes

Total Time: 18 minutes

Serves: 2

Calories: 411 kcal

Ingredients:

- 1 Cup of steel cut oats
- 3 Cups of coconut milk
- 4 Large honey crisp apples, sliced
- maple syrup
- Raisins

Cooking Instructions:

1. Except raisin, merge all the ingredients together. Place the mixture in the cooking trays with an even layer.
2. Lay the drip pan in the bottom of the cooking chamber. Select Air fry on the display panel.
3. Set the temperature to 360°F and adjust the cooking time to 13 minutes.
4. Press the start. When the display panel show "Add Food", put the cooking tray in the middle position.
5. When the unit show "turn food", ignore because the food is done. Top with raisin.
6. Serve and enjoy!!!

Spinach and Egg Casserole

Preparation Time: 10 minutes

Cook Time: 6 minutes

Total Time: 11 minutes

Serves: 4

Calories: 385 kcal

Ingredients:

- 1 Lb. cooked spinach
- 1 Can of cream of soup
- ¼ Cup of milk
- 6 Eggs, unbeaten
- 1 Cup of cheese, shredded

Cooking Instructions:

1. In a small mixing bowl, combine together the spinach, soup and milk together. Place the mixture in the cooking trays with an even layer.
2. Lay the drip pan in the bottom of the cooking chamber. Pour your eggs on top of the spinach mixture. Sprinkle cheese over the eggs.
3. Select Air fry on the display panel. Set the temperature to 380°F and adjust the cooking time to 6 minutes.
4. Press the start. When the display panel show "Add Food", put the cooking tray in the middle position.
5. When the unit show "turn food", ignore because the food is done.
6. Serve and enjoy!!!

Southwest Eggs

Preparation Time: 10 minutes

Cook Time: 10 minutes

Total Time: 20 minutes

Serves: 4

Calories: 217 kcal

Ingredients:

- 6 Eggs, scrambled
- EVOO
- 1 Tsp. butter
- 1 Tbsp. Garlic
- Filet
- Ro-Tel, drained
- ¼ Thyme
- Rosemary
- Salt and pepper
- Mozzarella
- Cheddar
- Tortilla
- Frozen hash brown triangle
- Salsa

Cooking Instructions:

1. Except the tortilla, harsh brown and salsa, combine all the ingredients together and put the mixture on the vortex cooking trays.
2. Add the tortilla, hash brown and fresh salsa. Lay the drip pan in the bottom of the cooking chamber.
3. Select Air fry on the display panel. Set the temperature to 375°F and adjust the cooking time to 10 minutes.
4. Press the start. When the display panel show "Add Food", put the cooking trays in the top and center position.
5. When the unit show "turn food", ignore because the food is done.
6. Serve and enjoy!!!

Shakshuka

Preparation Time: 10 minutes

Cook Time: 7 minutes

Total Time: 17 minutes

Serves: 4

Calories: 290 kcal

Ingredients:

- 1 Tbsp. olive oil
- 1 (14 Oz.) Can chickpeas
- ½ Red onion, diced
- 3 Cloves of garlic, minced
- 1 Tsp. cumin
- ½ Tsp. salt
- ¼ Tsp. red pepper flakes
- 1 (28 Oz.) Can crushed tomatoes
- 4 Large eggs
- 1 Oz. feta
- Parsley

Cooking Instructions:

1. In a small mixing bowl, merge together the chickpeas, onion, garlic, cumin, pepper flakes and salt. Stir it thoroughly and add tomatoes.
2. Beat the eggs on top. Place the mixture in the cooking trays with an even layer. Lay the drip pan in the bottom of the cooking chamber.
3. Select Air fry on the display panel. Set the temperature to 360°F and adjust the cooking time to 7 minutes.
4. Press the start. When the display panel show "Add Food", put the cooking tray in the middle position.
5. When the unit show "turn food", ignore because the food is done. Garnish with feta and parsley
6. Serve and enjoy!!!

Pumpkin Porridge

Preparation Time: 10 minutes

Cook Time: 15 minutes

Total Time: 25 minutes

Serves: 4

Calories: 385 kcal

Ingredients:

- 3 Cups of rolled oats
- 2 Cups of pumpkin, canned
- 1 Can evaporated milk
- 2 Duck eggs, or chicken
- 6 Cups of water
- 1 Cup of sugar
- Pumpkin pie spice

Cooking Instructions:

1. Combine all the ingredients together and place the mixture in the cooking trays with an even layer. Lay the drip pan in the bottom of the cooking chamber.
2. Select Air fry on the display panel. Set the temperature to 360°F and adjust the cooking time to 15 minutes.
3. Press the start. When the display panel show "Add Food", put the cooking tray in the middle position.
4. When the unit show "turn food", ignore because the food is done.
5. Serve and enjoy!!!

Quiche Boats

Preparation Time: 10 minutes

Cook Time: 10 minutes

Total Time: 20 minutes

Serves: 4

Calories: 117 kcal

Ingredients:

- 1 Packet of 'stand and stuff ' Old El Paso brand soft tacos
- 2 Eggs per taco 'boat' plus a dash of milk
- Any fillings of choice like chopped spinach, grated cheese, diced bacon, shallots, mushrooms

Cooking Instructions:

1. Chop all the fillings and add them to the boats. Add the egg/milk mixture and place the mixture in the cooking trays with an even layer.
2. Lay the drip pan in the bottom of the cooking chamber. Select Airfry on the display panel.
3. Set the temperature to 380°F and adjust the cooking time to 10 minutes.
4. Press the start. When the display panel show "Add Food", put the cooking tray in the middle position.
5. When the unit show "turn food", ignore because the food is done.
6. Serve and enjoy!!!

Omelet

Preparation Time: 10 minutes

Cook Time: 10 minutes

Total Time: 20 minutes

Serves: 4

Calories: 268 kcal

Ingredients:

- Bacon
- 6 Eggs
- Milk
- Pepper
- Cheese

Cooking Instructions:

1. In a small mixing bowl, combine together the eggs, milk, salt, pepper and bacon. Place the mixture in the cooking trays with an even layer.
2. Lay the drip pan in the bottom of the cooking chamber. Select Airfry on the display panel.
3. Set the temperature to 380°F and adjust the cooking time to 10 minutes.
4. Press the start. When the display panel show "Add Food", put the cooking tray in the center position.
5. When the unit show "turn food", ignore because the food is done. Top with cheese and fold over.
6. Serve and enjoy!!!

Mini Egg Muffins

Preparation Time: 10 minutes

Cook Time: 15 minutes

Total Time: 25 minutes

Serves: 4

Calories: 381 kcal

Ingredients:

- 2 Cooked sausage links
- 2 Egg yolks
- 1 Egg
- Splash of milk
- 3 Tbsp. chopped onion
- Shredded cheese

Cooking Instructions:

1. Combine together the eggs and milk. Spray 6 cups of muffin pan with non-stick spray. Put 2 cups of water in the vortex cooking tray and put the muffin cups.
2. Add sausage, onion into each cup. Pour egg mixture into each cup to fill. Top with shredded cheese.
3. Lay the drip pan in the bottom of the cooking chamber. Select Airfry on the display panel.
4. Set the temperature to 360°F and adjust the cooking time to 15 minutes.
5. Press the start. When the display panel show "Add Food", put the cooking tray in the center position.
6. When the unit show "turn food", ignore because the food is done.
7. Serve and enjoy!!!

INSTANT VORTEX AIR FRYER LUNCH RECIPES

Fall off the Bone Ribs

Preparation Time: 10 minutes

Cook Time: 25 minutes

Total Time: 35 minutes

Serves: 4

Calories: 197 kcal

Ingredients:

- 2 Racks of ribs
- 2 Cups of apple juice
- 1 Coors Light Beer
- 1 Cup of your favorite BBQ Sauce

Cooking Instructions:

1. In a medium mixing bowl, merge together the apple juice, beer and ribs meat. Place the mixture in the cooking tray.
2. Lay the drip pan in the bottom of the cooking chamber. Select Airfry on the display panel.
3. Set the temperature to 370°F and adjust the cooking time to 25 minutes.
4. Press the start. When the display panel show "Add Food", put the cooking tray in the center position.
5. When the unit show "turn food", ignore because the food is done.
6. Serve and enjoy!!!

Sweet Beet Chips

Preparation Time: 15 minutes

Cook Time: 40 minutes

Total Time: 55 minutes

Serves: 4

Calories: 430 kcal

Ingredients:

- 3 Medium red beets, peeled and cut into thick slices
- 2 Tsp. canola oil
- ¾ Tsp. kosher salt
- ¼ Tsp. black pepper

Cooking Instructions:

1. In a large mixing bowl, combine together the sliced beets, oil, salt, and pepper. Place the mixture in the cooking tray.
2. Lay the drip pan in the bottom of the cooking chamber. Select Airfry on the display panel.
3. Set the temperature to 370°F and adjust the cooking time to 40 minutes.
4. Press the start. When the display panel show "Add Food", put the cooking tray in the center position.
5. When the unit show "turn food", ignore because the food is done.
6. Serve and enjoy!!!

Whole-Wheat Pizzas

Preparation Time: 10 minutes

Cook Time: 5 minutes

Total Time: 15 minutes

Serves: 2

Calories: 118 kcal

Ingredients:

- ¼ Cup of marinara sauce
- 2 Whole-wheat pita rounds
- 1 Cup of baby spinach leaves
- 1 Small plum tomato, cut into 8 slices
- 1 Small garlic clove, sliced
- 1 Oz. mozzarella cheese, shredded
- ¼ Oz. shaved Parmigiano-Reggiano cheese

Cooking Instructions:

1. Apply marinara sauce equally over 1 side of each pita bread. Top with half each of the spinach leaves, tomato slices, garlic, and cheeses.
2. Place the pita in the cooking tray. Lay the drip pan in the bottom of the cooking chamber.
3. Select Air fry on the display panel. Set the temperature to 350°F and adjust the cooking time to 5 minutes.
4. Press the start. When the display panel show "Add Food", put the cooking tray in the center position.
5. When the unit show "turn food", ignore because the food is done.
6. Serve and enjoy!!!

Curry Chickpeas

Preparation Time: 10 minutes

Cook Time: 15 minutes

Total Time: 25 minutes

Serves: 4

Calories: 278 kcal

Ingredients:

- 1 (15 Oz.) Can of no-salt-added chickpeas, drained and rinsed
- 2 Tbsp. red wine vinegar
- 2 Tbsp. olive oil
- 2 Tsp. curry powder
- ½ Tsp. ground turmeric
- ¼ Tsp. ground coriander
- ¼ Tsp. ground cumin
- 2 Tsp. plus ground cinnamon
- ¼ Tsp. kosher salt
- ½ Tsp. Aleppo pepper
- Fresh cilantro, sliced

Cooking Instructions:

1. In a medium mixing bowl, smash chickpeas with your hands (do not crush); discard chickpea skins.
2. Put vinegar and oil to chickpeas and give it a nice stir. Put curry powder, turmeric, coriander, cumin, and cinnamon; mix thoroughly.
3. Place chickpeas in the cooking tray. Lay the drip pan in the bottom of the cooking chamber.
4. Select Air fry on the display panel. Set the temperature to 400°F and adjust the cooking time to 15 minutes.
5. Press the start. When the display panel show "Add Food", put the cooking tray in the center position.
6. When the unit show "turn food", ignore because the food is done. Transfer chickpeas to a bowl. Top with salt, Aleppo pepper, and cilantro.
7. Serve and enjoy!!!

INSTANT VORTEX AIR FRYER POULTRY RECIPES

Mississippi Roast Chicken Style

Preparation Time: 10 minutes

Cook Time: 20 minutes

Total Time: 30 minutes

Serves: 4

Calories: 438 kcal

Ingredients:

- 2 Large chicken breast, boneless, skinless
- Fresh green beans, washed
- Mini potatoes, washed
- 1 Packet powder chicken gravy mix
- 1 Packet powder ranch dressing mix
- 1 Tsp. minced garlic
- ¼ Cup of butter, cut
- ½ Cup of water

Cooking Instructions:

1. Combine all the ingredients together in a medium mixing bowl. Place the mixture in the cooking trays with an even layer.
2. Lay the drip pan in the bottom of the cooking chamber. Select Airfry on the display panel.
3. Set the temperature to 375°F and adjust the cooking time to 20 minutes. Press the start.
4. When the display panel show "Add Food", put the cooking tray in the center position. When the unit show "turn food", ignore because the food is done.
5. Serve and enjoy!

Mayo Fresh Herb Chicken

Preparation Time: 10 minutes

Cook Time: 1 hour 30 minutes

Total Time: 1 hour 40 minutes

Serves: 4

Calories: 339 kcal

Ingredients:

- 1 Whole chicken
- Sage and Rosemary, fresh sprigs
- ¾ Cup of mayonnaise
- ½ Bottle of Chardonnay wine

Cooking Instructions:

1. In a medium mixing bowl, merge together the herbs and mayonnaise. Put in the refrigerator for at least 2 hours.
2. Rub the mayo mixture under the skin and cook to your desired consistency. Lay the chicken in cooking tray.
3. Lay the drip pan in the bottom of the cooking chamber. Select Airfry on the display panel.
4. Set the temperature to 370°F and adjust the cooking time to 1 hour 30 minutes.
5. Press the start. When the display panel show "Add Food", put the cooking tray in the center position.
6. When the unit show "turn food", ignore because the food is done.
7. Serve and enjoy!!!

Mayo Parmesan Chicken

Preparation Time: 10 minutes

Cook Time: 1 hour 5 minutes

Total Time: 1 hour 15 minutes

Serves: 4

Calories: 221 kcal

Ingredients:

- Mayo Parmesan Chicken
- Chicken quarters
- Mayo
- Parmesan cheese
- Italian seasoned bread crumbs

Cooking Instructions:

1. Apply mayo on all the chicken pieces. Combine equal parts parmesan cheese and bread crumbs. Lay the chicken in cooking tray.
2. Lay the drip pan in the bottom of the cooking chamber. Select Airfry on the display panel.
3. Set the temperature to 385°F and adjust the cooking time to 1 hour 5 minutes.
4. Press the start. When the display panel show "Add Food", put the cooking tray in the center position.
5. When the unit show "turn food", ignore because the food is done.
6. Serve and enjoy!!!

McCormick Chicken Ole

Preparation Time: 10 minutes

Cook Time: 15 minutes

Total Time: 25 minutes

Serves: 4

Calories: 310 kcal

Ingredients:

- 1¼ Lb. chicken, cut in strips
- 1 Tbsp. of coconut oil
- 1 (15 Oz.) Can corn, drained
- 1 (15 Oz.) Can tomato sauce
- 1 (4 Oz.) Can chopped green chilies, not drained
- 2 Tbsp. chili powder
- 1 Tsp. onion powder
- Toppings:
- Tortilla chips
- Mexican cheese
- Green onions
- Sour cream

Cooking Instructions:

1. In a small mixing bowl, mix together all the ingredients. Lay the chicken in cooking tray. Lay the drip pan in the bottom of the cooking chamber.
2. Select Air fry on the display panel. Set the temperature to 375°F and adjust the cooking time to 15 minutes.
3. Press the start. When the display panel show "Add Food", put the cooking tray in the center position.
4. When the unit show "turn food", ignore because the food is done. Top with toppings of your choice.
5. Serve and enjoy!!!

Mediterranean Chicken

Preparation Time: 10 minutes

Cook Time: 30 minutes

Total Time: 40 minutes

Serves: 4

Calories: 375 kcal

Ingredients:

- 4 Boneless skinless chicken breasts
- Olive oil
- Steak seasoning
- 1 Can (14.5 Oz.) diced tomatoes
- 1 Can of green olives, drained
- 1 Can of garbanzo beans, drained
- 1 (8 Oz.) package crumbled feta
- Bunch of basil leaves

Cooking Instructions:

1. In a medium mixing bowl, mix together all the ingredients. Lay the chicken in cooking tray. Lay the drip pan in the bottom of the cooking chamber.
2. Select Air fry on the display panel. Set the temperature to 365°F and adjust the cooking time to 30 minutes.
3. Press the start. When the display panel show "Add Food", put the cooking tray in the center position.
4. When the unit show "turn food", ignore because the food is done. It goes with noodles or rice.
5. Serve and enjoy!!!

Lemon Greek Chicken

Preparation Time: 10 minutes

Cook Time: 30 minutes

Total Time: 40 minutes

Serves: 4

Calories: 425 kcal

Ingredients:

- 6 Boneless skinless chicken thighs
- ½ Cup of chicken broth
- ½ Tsp. salt
- ½ Tsp. pepper
- ½ Tsp. garlic powder
- 1 Tbsp. olive oil
- 1 Lemon thinly sliced
- ¼ Cup of pitted kalamata olives sliced
- 2 Cloves of garlic minced
- ½ Tsp. dried oregano
- 1 Cup of cooked orzo

Cooking Instructions:

1. Season both sides of the chicken with salt, pepper and garlic powder. Add the remaining ingredients on top of the chicken. Lay the chicken in cooking tray.
2. Lay the drip pan in the bottom of the cooking chamber. Select Airfry on the display panel.
3. Set the temperature to 370°F and adjust the cooking time to 30 minutes.
4. Press the start. When the display panel show "Add Food", put the cooking tray in the center position.
5. When the unit show "turn food", ignore because the food is done. It goes with rice or vermicelli.
6. Serve and enjoy!!!

Lemon Orange Chicken Breast

Preparation Time: 10 minutes

Cook Time: 10 minutes

Total Time: 20 minutes

Serves: 4

Calories: 330 kcal

Ingredients:

- 2 Chicken breasts cut in strips
- 1 Lemon, slice into circles
- 1 Orange, slice into circles
- 1 Can of cream of chicken soup
- Salt
- Pepper

Cooking Instructions:

1. In a medium mixing bowl, combine together the chicken and soup. Give it a nice stir. Top with lemon and orange slices.
2. Lay the chicken in cooking tray. Lay the drip pan in the bottom of the cooking chamber. Select Airfry on the display panel.
3. Set the temperature to 385°F and adjust the cooking time to 10 minutes. Press the start.
4. When the display panel show "Add Food", put the cooking tray in the center position.
5. When the unit show "turn food", ignore because the food is done.
6. Serve and enjoy!!!

Lemon Pepper Chicken

Preparation Time: 10 minutes

Cook Time: 20 minutes

Total Time: 30 minutes

Serves: 4

Calories: 220 kcal

Ingredients:

- 4 Chicken breasts
- 3 Lemons, sliced
- Salt
- Pepper
- Chicken stock

Cooking Instructions:

1. Rinse and Pat dry the chicken. Run your fingers between the skin and chicken. Put about 4 slices of lemon between the skin and the meat of the chicken.
2. Season with salt and pepper. Lay the chicken in cooking tray. Add 3 cups of chicken stock up to half way on the chicken. Put remaining lemon on top.
3. Lay the drip pan in the bottom of the cooking chamber. Select Airfry on the display panel.
4. Set the temperature to 375°F and adjust the cooking time to 20 minutes.
5. Press the start. When the display panel show "Add Food", put the cooking tray in the center position.
6. When the unit show "turn food", ignore because the food is done.
7. Serve and enjoy!!!

Moroccan Spiced Chicken Thighs

Preparation Time: 10 minutes

Cook Time: 40 minutes

Total Time: 50 minutes

Serves: 4

Calories: 268 kcal

Ingredients:

- 1 Tbsp. paprika
- 1 Tbsp. packed light brown sugar
- 2 Tsp. ground cumin
- 1 Tsp. ground cinnamon
- 1 Tsp. ground ginger
- 1 Tsp. salt
- 1 Tsp. garlic powder
- ¼ Tsp. ground black pepper
- ¼ Tsp. ground cayenne pepper
- 6 Bone-in chicken thighs

Cooking Instructions:

1. In a medium mixing bowl, merge together the paprika, brown sugar, cumin, cinnamon, ginger, salt, garlic powder, black pepper, and cayenne pepper.
2. Stir thoroughly and rub seasoning mixture over chicken thighs on all sides. Lay the chicken in cooking tray.
3. Lay the drip pan in the bottom of the cooking chamber. Select Airfry on the display panel.
4. Set the temperature to 385°F and adjust the cooking time to 40 minutes.
5. Press the start. When the display panel show "Add Food", put the cooking tray in the center position.
6. When the unit show "turn food", ignore because the food is done.
7. Serve and enjoy!!!

Japanese Style Chicken Curry

Preparation Time: 10 minutes

Cook Time: 30 minutes

Total Time: 40 minutes

Serves: 4

Calories: 260 kcal

Ingredients:

- 1 Lb. boneless skinless chicken thighs, cut into bite sized pieces
- Salt and pepper
- 2 Onions, sliced thin
- 2 Cloves of garlic, minced
- 3 Cups of unsalted chicken stock
- 2 Large carrots, peeled and sliced
- 2 Cups of diced potatoes
- Japanese curry roux
- Cooked rice

Cooking Instructions:

1. In a medium mixing bowl, combine all the ingredients together and mix properly to coat the chicken well. Lay the chicken in cooking tray.
2. Lay the drip pan in the bottom of the cooking chamber. Select Airfry on the display panel.
3. Set the temperature to 380°F and adjust the cooking time to 30 minutes.
4. Press the start. When the display panel show "Add Food", put the cooking tray in the center position.
5. When the unit show "turn food", ignore because the food is done.
6. Serve and enjoy!!!

INSTANT VORTEX AIR FRYER BEEF & PORK RECIPES

Brisket

Preparation Time: 10 minutes

Cook Time: 50 minutes

Total Time: 60 minutes

Serves: 4

Calories: 149 kcal

Ingredients:

- Brisket
- Stubs rub
- Stubs Chile marinade

Cooking Instructions:

1. In a small mixing bowl, mix together all the ingredients and keep it to marinade overnight.
2. The next day put the brisket in the cooking tray, top with some Stubb's Chile marinade
3. Lay the drip pan in the bottom of the cooking chamber. Select Airfry on the display panel.
4. Set the temperature to 370°F and adjust the cooking time to 50 minutes.
5. Press the start. When the display panel show "Add Food", put the cooking tray in the center position.
6. When the unit show "turn food", ignore because the food is done. Top with brisket salad with kale and fresh peaches.
7. Serve and enjoy!!!

Braising Steaks

Preparation Time: 10 minutes

Cook Time: 25 minutes

Total Time: 35 minutes

Serves: 4

Calories: 438 kcal

Ingredients:

- 2 Large pieces of braising steak, into strips
- 2 Tbsp. of seasoned flour
- 2 Cups of grated carrot
- 1 Cup of soy sauce
- ½ Cup of brown sugar
- ½ Cup of water
- Spring onions, chopped

Cooking Instructions:

1. Put the beef and flour into a zip lock bag. Shake the bag well. Place in the cooking tray and add carrots, soy sauce, brown sugar and water.
2. Lay the drip pan in the bottom of the cooking chamber. Select Airfry on the display panel.
3. Set the temperature to 390°F and adjust the cooking time to 25 minutes.
4. Press the start. When the display panel show "Add Food", put the cooking tray in the center position.
5. When the unit show "turn food", ignore because the food is done. Top with chopped spring onions.
6. Serve and enjoy!!!

Bottom Round Roast

Preparation Time: 10 minutes

Cook Time: 20 minutes

Total Time: 30 minutes

Serves: 4

Calories: 286 kcal

Ingredients:

- 3 Lbs. bottom round roast
- Marinade of choice
- Seasonings of choice
- 2 Cups of beef stock
- 1 Onion, quartered

Cooking Instructions:

1. Begin by marinating the roast for about 2 hours. Put 2 cups of beef stock and the onion to the cooking tray. Add the roast.
2. Lay the drip pan in the bottom of the cooking chamber. Select Airfry on the display panel.
3. Set the temperature to 390°F and adjust the cooking time to 20 minutes.
4. Press the start. When the display panel show "Add Food", put the cooking tray in the center position.
5. When the unit show "turn food", ignore because the food is done. Top with chopped spring onions.
6. Serve and enjoy!!!

Roast Beef

Preparation Time: 20 minutes

Cook Time: 55 minutes

Total Time: 1 hour 15 minutes

Serves: 8

Calories: 348 kcal

Ingredients:

- 1 Lb. fresh baby carrots
- 1 (4 Oz.) Can mushroom stems and pieces, drained
- 1 (3 Lbs.) Beef rump roast
- ½ Tsp. garlic powder
- ¼ Tsp. pepper
- 1 Tbsp. canola oil
- 1 (12 Oz.) Jar beef gravy
- 1 (10 ¾ Oz.) Can condensed cream of mushroom soup
- 1 Cup of water
- 1 Envelope onion soup mix

Cooking Instructions:

1. In a small mixing bowl, mix the garlic powder and black pepper and rub the mixture onto all sides of the roast.
2. Add oil to the cooking tray and place the mixture. Add carrots and mushroom pieces.
3. Lay the drip pan in the bottom of the cooking chamber. Select Airfry on the display panel.
4. Set the temperature to 390°F and adjust the cooking time to 55 minutes.
5. Press the start. When the display panel show "Add Food", put the cooking tray in the center position.
6. When the unit show "turn food", ignore because the food is done. Spoon the gravy over the meat and veggies.
7. Whisk together the gravy, soup, water, and soup mix in a bowl. Drizzle roast with the mixture.
8. Serve and enjoy!!!

Beef Wrapped Asparagus

Preparation Time: 10 minutes

Cook Time: 40 minutes

Total Time: 50 minutes

Serves: 4

Calories: 225 kcal

Ingredients:

- Large fresh asparagus, ends trimmed out
- Beef, thinly sliced
- Minced garlic
- Green onion, sliced
- Mushrooms
- 1 Can of cream of mushroom soup
- 1 Can of beef broth

Cooking Instructions:

1. Place the beef on the cooking tray and place asparagus and garlic on top. Roll the beef around asparagus.
2. Add onion and mushrooms. Mix the soup and beef broth together. Pour over all. Lay the drip pan in the bottom of the cooking chamber.
3. Select Air fry on the display panel. Set the temperature to 370°F and adjust the cooking time to 40 minutes.
4. Press the start. When the display panel show "Add Food", put the cooking tray in the center position.
5. When the unit show "turn food", ignore because the food is done.
6. Serve and enjoy!!!

Brown Gravy

Preparation Time: 10 minutes

Cook Time: 1 hour

Total Time: 1 hour 10 minutes

Serves: 4

Calories: 365 kcal

Ingredients:

- 1 Lb. Beef stew meat
- 1 Jar of brown gravy
- 3 Cups of noodles
- 1 Package of Lipton onion mix
- Enough Water to cover noodles

Cooking Instructions:

1. Combine all the ingredients together in a medium mixing bowl moving in this order: Lipton onion soup, gravy, water and noodles.
2. Place the mixture in the cooking tray. Lay the drip pan in the bottom of the cooking chamber.
3. Select Air fry on the display panel. Set the temperature to 360°F and adjust the cooking time to 1 hour 10 minutes.
4. Press the start. When the display panel show "Add Food", put the cooking tray in the center position.
5. When the unit show "turn food", ignore because the food is done. Top with chopped spring onions.
6. Serve and enjoy!!!

Beef Tips in Mushroom Sauce

Preparation Time: 10 minutes

Cook Time: 40 minutes

Total Time: 50 minutes

Serves: 3

Calories: 216 kcal

Ingredients:

- 2 Lbs. lean chuck, cut in pieces
- 1 Can of mushroom soup
- 1 Package of onion soup mix
- 1 Can of Diet Sprite

Cooking Instructions:

1. Place the meat in the cooking tray. Pour soup and onion mix over meat. Put Diet Sprit. Lay the drip pan in the bottom of the cooking chamber.
2. Select Air fry on the display panel. Set the temperature to 370°F and adjust the cooking time to 40 minutes.
3. Press the start. When the display panel show "Add Food", put the cooking tray in the center position.
4. When the unit show "turn food", ignore because the food is done. Top with any vegetables of choice.
5. Serve and enjoy!!!

BBQ Ribs

Preparation Time: 10 minutes

Cook Time: 50 minutes

Total Time: 60 minutes

Serves: 4

Calories: 396 kcal

Ingredients:

- 4 Lbs. Ribs of your choice
- 2 Tsp. Worcestershire sauce
- 1 Tsp. vinegar
- Salt to taste
- Pepper to taste
- 1 Bottle of sweet baby rays BBQ
- 2 Tbsp. brown sugar
- 1 Tsp. oregano

Cooking Instructions:

1. Except the ribs, combine together all the ingredients in a medium mixing bowl. Place the ribs in the cooking tray and pour the sauce over the ribs.
2. Lay the drip pan in the bottom of the cooking chamber. Select Airfry on the display panel.
3. Set the temperature to 375°F and adjust the cooking time to 50 minutes.
4. Press the start. When the display panel show "Add Food", put the cooking tray in the center position.
5. When the unit show "turn food", ignore because the food is done.
6. Serve and enjoy!!!

Creamy Ranch Pork Chops

Preparation Time: 10 minutes

Cook Time: 40 minutes

Total Time: 50 minutes

Serves: 4

Calories: 405 kcal

Ingredients:

- 4 Pork chops
- 2 Cans of cream of chicken soup
- 2 Packets of dry ranch salad dressing mix
- 1 Cup of milk
- 6 Medium potatoes, peeled and cut into chunks

Cooking Instructions:

1. Arrange the potatoes in the cooking tray. Put the pork chops on top of the potatoes.
2. In a large mixing bowl, merge together soup, salad dressing and milk. Pour over the other ingredients in the cooking tray.
3. Lay the drip pan in the bottom of the cooking chamber. Select Airfry on the display panel.
4. Set the temperature to 365°F and adjust the cooking time to 40 minutes.
5. Press the start. When the display panel show "Add Food", put the cooking tray in the center position.
6. When the unit show "turn food", ignore because the food is done.
7. Serve and enjoy!!!

INSTANT VORTEX AIR FRYER FISH & SEAFOOD RECIPES

Tomato Tilapia

Preparation Time: 10 minutes

Cook Time: 20 minutes

Total Time: 30 minutes

Serves: 4

Calories: 276 kcal

Ingredients:

- 6 Frozen Tilapia
- 2 Tomatoes, chopped and diced
- 2 Tbsp. drained capers
- 1 Clove of garlic, minced
- 1 Tbsp. basil
- ½ Tsp. salt
- ¾ Lb. fresh cut green beans
- 1 Cup of sweet peppers, diced

Cooking Instructions:

1. In a small mixing bowl, combine together the garlic, basil, salt, and capers. Stir properly.
2. Put the mixture in the cooking tray. Put the fish, pepper and tomatoes. Place the green beans on top of the fish.
3. Lay the drip pan in the bottom of the cooking chamber. Select Airfry on the display panel.
4. Set the temperature to 375°F and adjust the cooking time to 40 minutes.
5. Press the start. When the display panel show "Add Food", put the cooking tray in the center position.
6. When the unit show "turn food", ignore because the food is done. This goes with rice or egg noodles.
7. Serve and enjoy!!!

Shrimp with Mango Mango Preserves

Preparation Time: 10 minutes

Cook Time: 5 minutes

Total Time: 15 minutes

Serves: 2

Calories: 289 kcal

Ingredients:

- 1 Lb. Cooked shrimp
- 1 Tbsp. water
- 1 Tbsp. of Mango Preserves

Cooking Instructions:

1. In a small mixing bowl, add all the ingredients and stir to mix well. Place the mixture in the cooking tray.
2. Lay the drip pan in the bottom of the cooking chamber. Select Airfry on the display panel.
3. Set the temperature to 365°F and adjust the cooking time to 5 minutes.
4. Press the start. When the display panel show "Add Food", put the cooking tray in the center position.
5. When the unit show "turn food", ignore because the food is done. This goes with rice or pasta.
6. Serve and enjoy!!!

Shrimp Teriyaki

Preparation Time: 10 minutes

Cook Time: 15 minutes

Total Time: 25 minutes

Serves: 2

Calories: 388 kcal

Ingredients:

- 2 Lbs. of raw deveined and clean tail on jumbo shrimp
- 1 Medium onion make cuts about ¼ inch apart vertically
- 2 Handfuls of baby peppers, cut it vertically
- 2 Tsp. of olive oil
- 1 Jar of Teriyaki sauce

Cooking Instructions:

1. In a small mixing bowl, add all the ingredients except the teriyaki sauce. Stir to mix well. Place the mixture in the cooking tray.
2. Lay the drip pan in the bottom of the cooking chamber. Select Airfry on the display panel.
3. Set the temperature to 370°F and adjust the cooking time to 15 minutes.
4. Press the start. When the display panel show "Add Food", put the cooking tray in the center position.
5. When the unit show "turn food", ignore because the food is done. Add the teriyaki sauce. This goes with rice or lettuce.
6. Serve and enjoy!!!

Shrimp Scampi with Linguini

Preparation Time: 10 minutes

Cook Time: 40 minutes

Total Time: 50 minutes

Serves: 2

Calories: 232 kcal

Ingredients:

- Garlic powder
- Lemon pepper seasoning
- 4 Oz. grated cheese
- 4 Cups of water
- 1 Lb. of linguini
- 2 Boxes of frozen shrimp scampi

Cooking Instructions:

1. In a small mixing bowl, mix together the linguini and water. Stir properly. Place the mixture in the cooking tray. Add the shrimp.
2. Lay the drip pan in the bottom of the cooking chamber. Select Airfry on the display panel.
3. Set the temperature to 360°F and adjust the cooking time to 40 minutes.
4. Press the start. When the display panel show "Add Food", put the cooking tray in the center position.
5. When the unit show "turn food", ignore because the food is done. Top with cheese.
6. Serve and enjoy!!!

Boiled Shrimp

Preparation Time: 10 minutes

Cook Time: 25 minutes

Total Time: 35 minutes

Serves: 4

Calories: 185 kcal

Ingredients:

- 1 Large can of beer
- 1 Tbsp. Old Bay Seasoning
- 3 Bay leaves
- 12 Oz. bag of frozen raw shrimp with tails and shells
- 4 Oz. andouille sausage, cut into 4 pieces
- 4 Oz. Idaho potatoes, peeled and cut in half
- 2 Ears of corn, divided into two

Cooking Instructions:

1. In a small mixing bowl, put all the ingredients except the shrimp. Place the mixture in the cooking tray. Put the shrimp on top.
2. Lay the drip pan in the bottom of the cooking chamber. Select Airfry on the display panel.
3. Set the temperature to 365°F and adjust the cooking time to 25 minutes. Press the start.
4. When the display panel show "Add Food", put the cooking tray in the center position. When the unit show "turn food", ignore because the food is done.
5. Serve and enjoy!!!

Shrimp Scampi with Zucchini

Preparation Time: 10 minutes

Cook Time: 10 minutes

Total Time: 20 minutes

Serves: 4

Calories: 315 kcal

Ingredients:

- 2 Tbsp. unsalted butter
- 1 Lb. medium shrimp, peeled and deveined
- 3 Cloves garlic, minced
- ½ Tsp. red pepper flakes
- ¼ Cup of chicken stock
- Juice of 1 lemon
- Kosher salt to taste
- Freshly ground black pepper to taste
- 1½ Lb. zucchini, spiralized
- 2 Tbsp. freshly grated Parmesan
- 2 Tbsp. chopped fresh parsley leaves

Cooking Instructions:

1. Place the shrimp, garlic, butter, red pepper flakes in the cooking tray. Put chicken stock, lemon juice, salt and pepper. Add zucchini noodles and stir thoroughly.
2. Lay the drip pan in the bottom of the cooking chamber. Select Airfry on the display panel.
3. Set the temperature to 365°F and adjust the cooking time to 10 minutes.
4. Press the start. When the display panel show "Add Food", put the cooking tray in the center position.
5. When the unit show "turn food", ignore because the food is done. Top with parmesan and parsley.
6. Serve and enjoy!!!

Shrimp Linguine Alfredo

Preparation Time: 10 minutes

Cook Time: 20 minutes

Total Time: 30 minutes

Serves: 4

Calories: 196 kcal

Ingredients:

- 1 Lb. half and half
- 4 Tbsp. cream cheese
- 1 Cup of good grated parmesan
- 2 Tsp. garlic powder
- 2 Sticks unsalted butter
- 2 Bags of frozen cooked baby shrimp
- Linguine

Cooking Instructions:

1. Put butter, cream cheese, half and half, parmesan cheese, garlic powder and shrimp in the cooking tray.
2. Add salt and pepper to taste. Lay the drip pan in the bottom of the cooking chamber.
3. Select Air fry on the display panel. Set the temperature to 365°F and adjust the cooking time to 20 minutes.
4. Press the start. When the display panel show "Add Food", put the cooking tray in the center position.
5. When the unit show "turn food", ignore because the food is done. This goes with linguine pasta.
6. Serve and enjoy!!!

Shrimp Scampi

Preparation Time: 10 minutes

Cook Time: 20 minutes

Total Time: 30 minutes

Serves: 4

Calories: 246 kcal

Ingredients:

- 12 Oz. package of frozen shrimp, boiled, peeled and chopped
- 1 Pouch of the Campbell's shrimp scampi sauce
- 1 Pouch of water
- 2 Tbsp. of butter
- 2 Tbsp. minced fresh garlic
- 1 Tsp. onion powder
- A handful of spinach
- 3 Large mushrooms, chopped
- 1 Roasted red pepper, chopped
- 1 Lb. of angel hair noodles

Cooking Instructions:

1. In a small mixing bowl, put all the ingredients except the shrimp. Place the mixture in the cooking tray. Put the shrimp on top.
2. Lay the drip pan in the bottom of the cooking chamber. Select Airfry on the display panel.
3. Set the temperature to 385°F and adjust the cooking time to 20 minutes. Press the start.
4. When the display panel show "Add Food", put the cooking tray in the center position. When the unit show "turn food", ignore because the food is done.

INSTANT VORTEX AIR FRYER SOUP RECIPES

Super Quick Potato Soup

Preparation Time: 10 minutes

Cook Time: 25 minutes

Total Time: 35 minutes

Serves: 4

Calories: 270 kcal

Ingredients:

- 1 Package Bear Creek potato soup
- ½ Bag of fresh cut hash brown
- 4 Strips of bacon
- ½ Large onion
- 2 Cups of milk

Cooking Instructions:

1. In a large mixing bowl, combine together the bacon, onion, soup mix. Add the potatoes and milk. Place the mixture in the cooking tray.
2. Lay the drip pan in the bottom of the cooking chamber. Select Airfry on the display panel.
3. Set the temperature to 385°F and adjust the cooking time to 25 minutes.
4. Press the start. When the display panel show "Add Food", put the cooking tray in the center position.
5. When the unit show "turn food", ignore because the food is done. Top with shredded cheese.
6. Serve and enjoy!!!

Sweet Potato and Black Bean Chili

Preparation Time: 10 minutes

Cook Time: 35 minutes

Total Time: 45 minutes

Serves: 4

Calories: 328 kcal

Ingredients:

- 3 Bacon strips, chopped
- 1 Large sweet onion, chopped
- 6 Garlic cloves, minced
- 1 (14.5 Oz.) Can of diced tomatoes
- 1 Medium sweet potato, peeled and diced
- 4 (15 Oz.) Cans of black beans, rinsed and drained
- 2 Tbsp. ketchup
- 2 Tsp. Worcestershire sauce
- 1 Tbsp. chili powder
- 1 Tsp. cumin
- 2 Cups of chicken broth
- 2 Cups of water
- 1 Bunch cilantro, roughly chopped
- 1 Lime, juiced
- Salt
- Fresh ground black pepper

Cooking Instructions:

1. In a large mixing bowl, combine together the bacon, onions, garlic, Tomatoes, sweet potatoes, beans, ketchup, Worcestershire sauce.
2. Add chili powder, cumin, chicken broth, water, salt and pepper. Give it a nice stir. Place the mixture in the cooking tray and top with cilantro and lime juice.
3. Lay the drip pan in the bottom of the cooking chamber. Select Airfry on the display panel.
4. Set the temperature to 380°F and adjust the cooking time to 35 minutes.

5. Press the start. When the display panel show "Add Food", put the cooking tray in the center position.
6. When the unit show "turn food", ignore because the food is done. Puree 2 cups of chili in a food processor.
7. Add the mixture to the cooking tray. Top with cheddar cheese, green onions, sour cream and avocado.
8. Serve and enjoy!!!

Sweet Potato Chili

Preparation Time: 10 minutes

Cook Time: 45 minutes

Total Time: 55 minutes

Serves: 4

Calories: 189 kcal

Ingredients:

- 2 (15 Oz.) Cans black beans, rinsed
- 4 (4 Oz.) Cans of diced green chilis with liquid
- 2 (28 Oz.) Cans of diced tomatoes with liquid
- 4 Cloves garlic, minced
- 1 White onion, diced
- 1 Large sweet potato, sliced into bite size pieces
- 4 Lbs. chicken tenderloins, sliced into bite size pieces
- 1 Packet of mild taco seasoning
- Juice from 1 fresh lime

Cooking Instructions:

1. In a medium mixing bowl, mix together all the ingredients. Stir thoroughly. Place the mixture in the cooking tray.
2. Lay the drip pan in the bottom of the cooking chamber. Select Airfry on the display panel.
3. Set the temperature to 380°F and adjust the cooking time to 45 minutes.
4. Press the start. When the display panel show "Add Food", put the cooking tray in the center position.
5. When the unit show "turn food", ignore because the food is done. Top with cheese or avocado.
6. Serve and enjoy!!!

Sweet Potato Lentil Soup

Preparation Time: 10 minutes

Cook Time: 1 hour

Total Time: 1 hour 10 minutes

Serves: 4

Calories: 312 kcal

Ingredients:

- 2 Tbsp. olive oil
- 1 Large onion, chopped
- 3 Cloves garlic, minced
- 1 Large carrot, peeled and chopped
- 1 Large sweet potato, peeled and cut into cubes
- 8 Cups of chicken broth
- 2 Cups of dried lentils
- 1 Can of (14.5 Oz.) diced tomatoes
- 1 Tsp. dried oregano leaves, crushed
- 1 Tsp. salt
- ¼ Tsp. ground black pepper
- 1 Can of (15 Oz.) Chickpeas, undrained

Cooking Instructions:

1. Pour oil into the cooking tray. Add all the ingredients together in a medium mixing bowl. Mix well.
2. Put the mixture into the cooking tray and place the chickpeas on top. Lay the drip pan in the bottom of the cooking chamber.
3. Select Air fry on the display panel. Set the temperature to 380°F and adjust the cooking time to 60 minutes.
4. Press the start. When the display panel show "Add Food", put the cooking tray in the center position.
5. When the unit show "turn food", ignore because the food is done.
6. Serve and enjoy!!!

Stuffed Pepper Soup

Preparation Time: 10 minutes

Cook Time: 45 minutes

Total Time: 55 minutes

Serves: 4

Calories: 412 kcal

Ingredients:

- 1 Lb. ground beef
- 1 Green pepper, diced
- 1 Onion, diced
- 1 (8 Oz.) Can crushed tomatoes
- 28 OZ. water
- 2 Tbsp. beef bouillon
- Salt
- Pepper
- Garlic
- Red pepper flakes
- 1½ Cups of cooked rice

Cooking Instructions:

1. In a small mixing bowl, combine all the ingredients and stir thoroughly. Lay the drip pan in the bottom of the cooking chamber.
2. Select Air fry on the display panel. Set the temperature to 370°F and adjust the cooking time to 45 minutes.
3. Press the start. When the display panel show "Add Food", put the cooking tray in the center position.
4. When the unit show "turn food", ignore because the food is done. Add the cooked rice.
5. Serve and enjoy!!!

Spinach and Ravioli Soup

Preparation Time: 10 minutes

Cook Time: 40 minutes

Total Time: 50 minutes

Serves: 4

Calories: 330 kcal

Ingredients:

- 1 (32 Oz.) Box of chicken broth
- 2 Cans of Italian diced tomatoes
- 1 Box of cream cheese
- 1 Bag of baby spinach
- 1 Bag of ravioli

Cooking Instructions:

1. In a large mixing bowl, combine together all the ingredients. Lay the drip pan in the bottom of the cooking chamber.
2. Select Air fry on the display panel. Set the temperature to 380°F and adjust the cooking time to 40 minutes.
3. Press the start. When the display panel show "Add Food", put the cooking tray in the center position.
4. When the unit show "turn food", ignore because the food is done.
5. Serve and enjoy!!!

Split Pea Soup

Preparation Time: 10 minutes

Cook Time: 60 minutes

Total Time: 1 hour 10 minutes

Serves: 4

Calories: 235 kcal

Ingredients:

- 16 Oz. Dried split peas
- 1½ Lb. ham bone
- 3 Carrots, diced
- 1 Yellow onion, diced
- 1 Shallot, diced
- 2 Stalks celery, diced
- 3 Cloves of garlic, minced
- 2 Potatoes, diced
- Nutmeg to taste
- Parsley to taste
- 1 Tsp. dried thyme
- ½ Tsp. ground black pepper
- 1 Bay leaf
- 7 Cups of low sodium chicken stock chicken

Cooking Instructions:

1. In a large mixing bowl, mix together the split peas, carrots, yellow onion, shallot, celery, garlic, thyme, pepper, potatoes, nutmeg, parsley, bay leaf, and chicken stock. Stir thoroughly.
2. Place the mixture in the cooking tray. Add the ham bone on top. Lay the drip pan in the bottom of the cooking chamber.
3. Select Air fry on the display panel. Set the temperature to 380°F and adjust the cooking time to 60 minutes.
4. Press the start. When the display panel show "Add Food", put the cooking tray in the center position.
5. When the unit show "turn food", ignore because the food is done. Serve!

Spaghetti Sauce with Meat

Preparation Time: 10 minutes

Cook Time: 60 minutes

Total Time: 1 hour 10 minutes

Serves: 4

Calories: 335 kcal

Ingredients:

- 2 Lbs. ground beef
- 4 Cloves of garlic, minced
- 2 (28 Oz.) Cans of crushed tomatoes
- 1 (28 Oz.) Can of tomato sauce
- 1 Small can tomato paste
- 2 Tbsp. Fresh parsley, chopped
- 1 Tbsp. Sugar
- Salt to taste
- Pepper to taste

Cooking Instructions:

1. In a large mixing bowl, combine together all the ingredients. Place the mixture in the cooking tray. Lay the drip pan in the bottom of the cooking chamber.
2. Select Air fry on the display panel. Set the temperature to 380°F and adjust the cooking time to 60 minutes.
3. Press the start. When the display panel show "Add Food", put the cooking tray in the center position.
4. When the unit show "turn food", ignore because the food is done.
5. Serve and enjoy!!!

INSTANT VORTEX AIR FRYER RICE & PASTA RECIPES

Spanish Rice

Preparation Time: 10 minutes

Cook Time: 40 minutes

Total Time: 50 minutes

Serves: 4

Calories: 187 kcal

Ingredients:

- 1 Lb. of smoked cheddar cheese sausage, cut into small pieces
- 2 Cans (14½ Oz. each) Diced tomatoes, undrained
- 4 Cups of water
- 2 Cups of uncooked converted rice
- 1 Cup of salsa
- 1 Medium onion, chopped
- ½ Cup of green pepper, chopped
- ½ Cup of red pepper, chopped
- 4 Oz. can chopped green chilies
- 1 Envelope taco seasoning

Cooking Instructions:

1. In a large mixing bowl, combine together all the ingredients. Place the mixture in the cooking tray. Lay the drip pan in the bottom of the cooking chamber.
2. Select Air fry on the display panel. Set the temperature to 370°F and adjust the cooking time to 40 minutes.
3. Press the start. When the display panel show "Add Food", put the cooking tray in the center position.
4. When the unit show "turn food", ignore because the food is done.
5. Serve and enjoy!!!

Frito Enchilada Casserole

Preparation Time: 10 minutes

Cook Time: 5 minutes

Total Time: 15 minutes

Serves: 2

Calories: 311 kcal

Ingredients:

- 1 Lb. hamburger
- 1 Taco seasoning packet
- 2 Cup of Fritos
- 1 (10 Oz.) can enchilada sauce
- 2 Cup of shredded cheddar cheese

Cooking Instructions:

1. Put all the ingredients into the cooking tray in this order: hamburger, taco seasoning, Fritos, cheese and enchilada sauce.
2. Lay the drip pan in the bottom of the cooking chamber. Select Airfry on the display panel.
3. Set the temperature to 370°F and adjust the cooking time to 5 minutes.
4. Press the start. When the display panel show "Add Food", put the cooking tray in the center position.
5. When the unit show "turn food", ignore because the food is done.
6. Serve and enjoy!!!

Frozen Stuffed Shells with Frozen Italian Sausage

Preparation Time: 10 minutes

Cook Time: 40 minutes

Total Time: 50 minutes

Serves: 4

Calories: 297 kcal

Ingredients:

- 16 Frozen Stuffed Shells
- 7 Frozen Italian Sausage
- 30 Homemade Meat Balls
- 2 24 Oz. jars of sauce
- ½ Jar of water

Cooking Instructions:

1. Put enough sauce into the cooking tray. Layer the shells first, add more sauce, Italian sausage, sauce, and meatballs. Top with sauce.
2. Lay the drip pan in the bottom of the cooking chamber. Select Airfry on the display panel.
3. Set the temperature to 370°F and adjust the cooking time to 40 minutes.
4. Press the start. When the display panel show "Add Food", put the cooking tray in the center position.
5. When the unit show "turn food", ignore because the food is done.
6. Serve and enjoy!!!

Swedish Meatballs & Medium Shells with Alfredo Sauce

Preparation Time: 10 minutes

Cook Time: 25 minutes

Total Time: 35 minutes

Serves: 2

Calories: 397 kcal

Ingredients:

- 4 Cups of water
- 1 Lb. medium shells
- 1 Jar (28 Oz.) Alfredo sauce
- 1 Package (24 Oz.) frozen Swedish meatballs

Cooking Instructions:

1. In a large mixing bowl, put the water, pasta, sauce and meatballs. Stir thoroughly. Put the mixture in the cooking tray.
2. Lay the drip pan in the bottom of the cooking chamber. Select Airfry on the display panel.
3. Set the temperature to 350°F and adjust the cooking time to 25 minutes.
4. Press the start. When the display panel show "Add Food", put the cooking tray in the center position.
5. When the unit show "turn food", ignore because the food is done.
6. Serve and enjoy!!!

Sweet Potato Enchilada Casserole

Preparation Time: 10 minutes

Cook Time: 20 minutes

Total Time: 30 minutes

Serves: 4

Calories: 410 kcal

Ingredients:

- 1 Tbsp. olive oil
- 1 Small onion, diced
- 8 Oz. sweet potato noodles
- 1 Tbsp. minced garlic
- 1 Can of black beans, drained
- 1 Can of corn kernels
- 1 Can of enchilada sauce
- 1 Cup of shredded cheese
- 2 Cups of cooked chopped chicken

Cooking Instructions:

1. In a large mixing bowl, merge together the onions, sweet potato noodles, garlic and the remaining ingredients. Stir it properly.
2. Place the mixture in the cooking tray. Lay the drip pan in the bottom of the cooking chamber.
3. Select Air fry on the display panel. Set the temperature to 350°F and adjust the cooking time to 20 minutes.
4. Press the start. When the display panel show "Add Food", put the cooking tray in the center position.
5. When the unit show "turn food", ignore because the food is done. Top with tortilla chips and sour cream.
6. Serve and enjoy!!!

Spinach Artichoke Pasta

Preparation Time: 10 minutes

Cook Time: 10 minutes

Total Time: 20 minutes

Serves: 4

Calories: 369 kcal

Ingredients:

- 1 (10 Oz.) Box of frozen spinach
- 1 (13 Oz.) Can of artichoke hearts, chopped
- 2 Garlic cloves, minced
- 2 Tbsp. butter
- Salt to taste
- Pepper to taste
- 3 Cups of milk
- 2 Cups of pasta
- 2 ½ Cups shredded cheese

Cooking Instructions:

1. In a large mixing bowl, mix together the spinach, butter, artichoke, garlic, salt, pepper, milk, noodles and cheese. Give it a nice stir.
2. Put the mixture in the cooking tray. Lay the drip pan in the bottom of the cooking chamber. Select Airfry on the display panel.
3. Set the temperature to 350°F and adjust the cooking time to 10 minutes.
4. Press the start. When the display panel show "Add Food", put the cooking tray in the center position.
5. When the unit show "turn food", ignore because the food is done. Top with tortilla chips and sour cream.
6. Serve and enjoy!!!

Spinach Pesto Pasta

Preparation Time: 10 minutes

Cook Time: 5 minutes

Total Time: 15 minutes

Serves: 3

Calories: 282 kcal

Ingredients:

- 1 Lb. precooked noodles
- 1 Box of frozen spinach
- ½ Cup of butter
- ½ Cup of bagged Parmesan cheese
- 1 Tbsp. Parmesan
- ½ Pint of heavy cream
- 2 Tbsp. pesto

Cooking Instructions:

1. In a large mixing bowl, combine together all the ingredients. Place the mixture in the cooking tray. Lay the drip pan in the bottom of the cooking chamber.
2. Select Air fry on the display panel. Set the temperature to 320°F and adjust the cooking time to 5 minutes.
3. Press the start. When the display panel show "Add Food", put the cooking tray in the center position.
4. When the unit show "turn food", ignore because the food is done.
5. Serve and enjoy!!!

Spicy Sausage Pasta

Preparation Time: 10 minutes

Cook Time: 25 minutes

Total Time: 35 minutes

Serves: 4

Calories: 364 kcal

Ingredients:

- 1 Tbsp. olive oil
- 1 Lb. smoked sausage
- 1½ Cups of diced onion
- 2 Cloves of garlic, minced
- 2 Cups of chicken broth
- 1 (10 Oz.) Can of Ro-Tel tomatoes and green chiles, Mild
- ½ Cup heavy cream
- 8 Oz. penne pasta
- ½ Tsp. salt and pepper, each
- 1 Cup of Monterey Jack cheese, shredded
- ⅓ Cup of thinly sliced scallions

Cooking Instructions:

1. Spray the cooking tray with oil. In a small mixing bowl, mix together the sausage, onions, garlic.
2. Add broth, tomatoes, cream, pasta, salt and pepper. Give it a nice stir. Lay the drip pan in the bottom of the cooking chamber.
3. Select the Air fry on the display panel. Set the temperature to 360°F and adjust the cooking time to 25 minutes.
4. Press the start. When the display panel show "Add Food", put the cooking tray in the center position.
5. When the unit show "turn food", ignore because the food is done. Top with remaining cheese and sprinkle with scallions.
6. Serve and enjoy!!!

INSTANT VORTEX AIR FRYER VEGETABLE RECIPES

Stuffed Peppers with Turkey

Preparation Time: 10 minutes

Cook Time: 20 minutes

Total Time: 30 minutes

Serves: 4

Calories: 363 kcal

Ingredients:

- 2 Packages of Perdue, raw
- 8 Peppers
- ½ Cup of cooked rice, cooled
- ½ Onion, chopped
- 2 Eggs
- Dash of Worcestershire sauce
- Milk
- Ketchup
- Salt to taste
- Pepper to taste
- 24 Oz. Jar of spaghetti sauce
- ¼ Jar of water

Cooking Instructions:

1. In a small mixing bowl, combine together all the ingredients except spaghetti sauce and water. Put the mixture in the cooking tray. Add the sauce and water.
2. Lay the drip pan in the bottom of the cooking chamber. Select the Airfry on the display panel.
3. Set the temperature to 375°F and adjust the cooking time to 20 minutes.
4. Press the start. When the display panel show "Add Food", put the cooking tray in the center position.
5. When the unit show "turn food", ignore because the food is done. Top with remaining cheese and sprinkle with scallions.
6. Serve and enjoy!!!

Stuffed Portobello Mushrooms

Preparation Time: 10 minutes

Cook Time: 5 minutes

Total Time: 15 minutes

Serves: 2

Calories: 208 kcal

Ingredients:

- 6 Portobello mushrooms
- 1 Tbsp. Bruschetta
- 1 Tbsp. mozzarella cheese

Cooking Instructions:

1. Please the mushroom on the cooking tray. Stuff with a scoop of bruschetta and sprinkle with mozzarella cheese.
2. Lay the drip pan in the bottom of the cooking chamber. Select the Airfry on the display panel.
3. Set the temperature to 360°F and adjust the cooking time to 5 minutes.
4. Press the start. When the display panel show "Add Food", put the cooking tray in the center position.
5. When the unit show "turn food", ignore because the food is done.
6. Serve and enjoy!!!

Stuffed Zucchini

Preparation Time: 10 minutes

Cook Time: 25 minutes

Total Time: 35 minutes

Serves: 4

Calories: 368 kcal

Ingredients:

- Zucchini, cut in half lengthwise
- 1 Package of Mix Italian seasoning
- Fresh garlic
- parmesan cheese
- Olive oil
- Mozzarella cheese

Cooking Instructions:

1. Spoon a small amount of zucchini out and keep aside. In a small mixing bowl, mix together the zucchini, Italian seasoning, garlic and Parmesan cheese.
2. Drizzle small amount of olive oil on the zucchini and add back the reserved zucchini. Top with mozzarella cheese.
3. Put the mixture into the cooking tray. Lay the drip pan in the bottom of the cooking chamber.
4. Select the Air fry on the display panel. Set the temperature to 375°F and adjust the cooking time to 25 minutes.
5. Press the start. When the display panel show "Add Food", put the cooking tray in the center position.
6. When the unit show "turn food", ignore because the food is done.
7. Serve and enjoy!!!

Stuffed Zucchini Boats

Preparation Time: 10 minutes

Cook Time: 55 minutes

Total Time: 1 hour 5 minutes

Serves: 4

Calories: 285 kcal

Ingredients:

- 1 Medium zucchini, cut lengthwise and seeds removed
- 1 Lb. very lean hamburger
- ¼ Lb. Italian sausage
- ¾ Cup of onion, diced
- Salt to taste
- Pepper to taste

Cooking Instructions:

1. In a medium mixing bowl, merge together the hamburger, sausage, onion and zucchini seeds.
2. Line the cooking tray with foil and fill the zucchini halves with the meat mixture. Place them into the cooking tray.
3. Lay the drip pan in the bottom of the cooking chamber. Select the Airfry on the display panel.
4. Set the temperature to 350°F and adjust the cooking time to 55 minutes.
5. Press the start. When the display panel show "Add Food", put the cooking tray in the center position.
6. When the unit show "turn food", ignore because the food is done. This can absolutely go with baked potatoes.
7. Serve and enjoy!!!

Jimmy's Crack Slaw

Preparation Time: 10 minutes

Cook Time: 30 minutes

Total Time: 40 minutes

Serves: 4

Calories: 195 kcal

Ingredients:

- Bacon
- 2 Lbs. ground beef
- Salt
- Pepper
- Cabbage

Cooking Instructions:

1. In a large mixing bowl, combine together all the ingredients. Mix well and place the mixture in the cooking tray.
2. Lay the drip pan in the bottom of the cooking chamber. Select the Airfry on the display panel.
3. Set the temperature to 375°F and adjust the cooking time to 30 minutes.
4. Press the start. When the display panel show "Add Food", put the cooking tray in the center position.
5. When the unit show "turn food", ignore because the food is done.
6. Serve and enjoy!!!

Kale and Garlic

Preparation Time: 10 minutes

Cook Time: 10 minutes

Total Time: 20 minutes

Serves: 4

Calories: 321 kcal

Ingredients:

- ½ Lb. of fresh kale, chopped
- 4 Tbsp. of olive oil
- ¼ Cup of minced garlic
- 1 Tbsp. of salt
- 1 Tbsp. of black pepper

Cooking Instructions:

1. Spray the cooking tray with olive oil and put kale. Sprinkles more Olive oil on the kale. Add salt and pepper. Mix them all together.
2. Lay the drip pan in the bottom of the cooking chamber. Select the Airfry on the display panel.
3. Set the temperature to 365°F and adjust the cooking time to 10 minutes.
4. Press the start. When the display panel show "Add Food", put the cooking tray in the center position.
5. When the unit show "turn food", ignore because the food is done.
6. Serve and enjoy!!!

Ore-Ida Zesty Texas Cut Fries and Tater Tots

Preparation Time: 10 minutes

Cook Time: 40 minutes

Total Time: 50 minutes

Serves: 2

Calories: 190 kcal

Ingredients:

- 4 Lbs. Ore-Ida Zesty, sliced
- 2 Lbs. Tater Tots

Cooking Instructions:

1. Place all the ingredients in the cooking tray. Lay the drip pan in the bottom of the cooking chamber.
2. Select the Air fry on the display panel. Set the temperature to 380°F and adjust the cooking time to 40 minutes.
3. Press the start. When the display panel show "Add Food", put the cooking tray in the center position.
4. When the unit show "turn food", ignore because the food is done.
5. Serve and enjoy!!!

Pierogies

Preparation Time: 10 minutes

Cook Time: 20 minutes

Total Time: 30 minutes

Serves: 2

Calories: 295 kcal

Ingredients:

- 1 Medium onion
- 1 Clove of garlic
- 1 Bag of frozen pierogies
- 2 Tbsp. Parmesan cheese
- Salt to taste
- Pepper to taste
- Mozzarella cheese

Cooking Instructions:

1. In a large mixing bowl, mix together all the ingredients. Stir thoroughly. Lay the drip pan in the bottom of the cooking chamber.
2. Select the Air fry on the display panel. Set the temperature to 370°F and adjust the cooking time to 20 minutes.
3. Press the start. When the display panel show "Add Food", put the cooking tray in the center position.
4. When the unit show "turn food", ignore because the food is done.
5. Serve and enjoy!!!

INSTANT VORTEX AIR FRYER APPETIZER RECIPES

Spinach Artichoke Dip

Preparation Time: 10 minutes

Cook Time: 30 minutes

Total Time: 40 minutes

Serves: 3

Calories: 280 kcal

Ingredients:

- 10 Oz. frozen package chopped spinach-thawed and squeezed dry
- 14 Oz. jar artichoke hearts chopped
- 16 Oz. jar Ragu 4 cheese sauce
- 4 Oz. room temperature cream cheese
- ½ Cup of mozzarella cheese-grated
- 1 Cup of Parmesan cheese
- 1 Tsp. minced garlic

Cooking Instructions:

1. In a medium mixing bowl, mix all the ingredients together. Stir to combine and put the mixture in the cooking tray.
2. Lay the drip pan in the bottom of the cooking chamber. Select the Airfry on the display panel.
3. Set the temperature to 365°F and adjust the cooking time to 30 minutes.
4. Press the start. When the display panel show "Add Food", put the cooking tray in the center position.
5. When the unit show "turn food", ignore because the food is done. This goes with toasted bread slices or crackers.
6. Serve and enjoy!!!

Totino's Frozen Party Pizza

Preparation Time: 10 minutes

Cook Time: 28 minutes

Total Time: 38 minutes

Serves: 2

Calories: 193 kcal

Ingredients:

- Pizza
- McCormick's Italian Herb Seasoning

Cooking Instructions:

1. Place the pizza in the cooking tray and season with the Italian seasoning. Lay the drip pan in the bottom of the cooking chamber.
2. Select the Air fry on the display panel. Set the temperature to 350°F and adjust the cooking time to 28 minutes.
3. Press the start. When the display panel show "Add Food", put the cooking tray in the center position.
4. When the unit show "turn food", ignore because the food is done.
5. Serve and enjoy!!!

White Castle Frozen Burgers

Preparation Time: 10 minutes

Cook Time: 10 minutes

Total Time: 20 minutes

Serves: 2

Calories: 223 kcal

Ingredients:

- 1 Cup of water
- White Castle Burgers

Cooking Instructions:

1. Put small water and sandwiches in the cooking tray. Lay the drip pan in the bottom of the cooking chamber.
2. Select the Air fry on the display panel. Set the temperature to 375°F and adjust the cooking time to 10 minutes.
3. Press the start. When the display panel show "Add Food", put the cooking tray in the center position.
4. When the unit show "turn food", ignore because the food is done.
5. Serve and enjoy!!!

Queso

Preparation Time: 10 minutes

Cook Time: 10 minutes

Total Time: 20 minutes

Serves: 4

Calories: 323 kcal

Ingredients:

- 1 (32 Oz.) Block of Velveeta Cheese
- 1 (8 Oz. Package) Package of Cream Cheese
- 1 (10 Oz. Can) Can of Ro*Tel
- 1 (10 Oz. Can) Can of Cream Of Mushroom Soup
- 1 Lb. Ground Beef

Cooking Instructions:

1. In a medium mixing bowl, merge together the meat, Velveeta, cream cheese, soup and Ro Tel. Stir to combine. Place the mixture in the cooking tray.
2. Lay the drip pan in the bottom of the cooking chamber. Select the Airfry on the display panel.
3. Set the temperature to 370°F and adjust the cooking time to 10 minutes.
4. Press the start. When the display panel show "Add Food", put the cooking tray in the center position.
5. When the unit show "turn food", ignore because the food is done.
6. Serve and enjoy!!!

Teriyaki Chicken Wings

Preparation Time: 10 minutes

Cook Time: 40 minutes

Total Time: 50 minutes

Serves: 2

Calories: 269 kcal

Ingredients:

- 2½ Lbs. Frozen wings
- ¼ Cup of Kikkoman Teriyaki Sauce

Cooking Instructions:

1. In a small mixing bowl, mix together the two ingredients. Put into the cooking tray. Lay the drip pan in the bottom of the cooking chamber.
2. Select the Air fry on the display panel. Set the temperature to 360°F and adjust the cooking time to 40 minutes.
3. Press the start. When the display panel show "Add Food", put the cooking tray in the center position.
4. When the unit show "turn food", ignore because the food is done.
5. Serve and enjoy!!!

Sweet and Sour Meatballs

Preparation Time: 10 minutes

Cook Time: 45 minutes

Total Time: 55 minutes

Serves: 4

Calories: 350 kcal

Ingredients:

- 10 Oz. Chili sauce
- 16 Oz. Grape jelly
- 2 Lbs. frozen meatballs

Cooking Instructions:

1. In a small mixing bowl, mix together the chili sauce and grape jelly. Add the meatballs and sauce. Give it a nice stir. Put the mixture into the cooking tray.
2. Lay the drip pan in the bottom of the cooking chamber. Select the Airfry on the display panel.
3. Set the temperature to 380°F and adjust the cooking time to 45 minutes.
4. Press the start. When the display panel show "Add Food", put the cooking tray in the center position.
5. When the unit show "turn food", ignore because the food is done.
6. Serve and enjoy!!!

Tamale Dip

Preparation Time: 10 minutes

Cook Time: 30 minutes

Total Time: 40 minutes

Serves: 4

Calories: 250 kcal

Ingredients:

- 1 28 Oz. Can of whole tomatoes
- 1 15 Oz. Can of tomato sauce
- 1 Large onion
- 2 Tbsp. chili powder
- 1 Tbsp. garlic powder
- Salt to taste
- Pepper to taste
- 2 Cans of tamales
- 1 Can of drained sliced black olives

Cooking Instructions:

1. In a food processor, blend tomatoes, sauce and spices your desired consistency. Put the mixture in the cooking tray.
2. Lay the drip pan in the bottom of the cooking chamber. Select the Airfry on the display panel.
3. Set the temperature to 380°F and adjust the cooking time to 30 minutes.
4. Press the start. When the display panel show "Add Food", put the cooking tray in the center position.
5. When the unit show "turn food", ignore because the food is done. Slice the tamales and stir into sauce and add black olives.
6. Serve and enjoy!!!

Spinach Artichoke Dip

Preparation Time: 10 minutes

Cook Time: 30 minutes

Total Time: 40 minutes

Serves: 4

Calories: 410 kcal

Ingredients:

- 10 Oz. Frozen package spinach, chopped, thawed and squeezed dry
- 14 Oz. Jar of artichoke hearts chopped
- 16 Oz. Jar of Ragu 4 cheese sauce
- 4 Oz. Cream cheese
- ½ Cup of mozzarella cheese, grated
- 1 Cup of Parmesan cheese
- 1 Tsp. minced garlic

Cooking Instructions:

1. In a medium mixing bowl, mix all the ingredients together. Stir to combine and put the mixture in the cooking tray.
2. Lay the drip pan in the bottom of the cooking chamber. Select the Airfry on the display panel.
3. Set the temperature to 365°F and adjust the cooking time to 30 minutes.
4. Press the start. When the display panel show "Add Food", put the cooking tray in the center position.
5. When the unit show "turn food", ignore because the food is done. This goes with toasted bread slices or crackers.
6. Serve and enjoy!!!

Steak and Beef Nachos

Preparation Time: 10 minutes

Cook Time: 5 minutes

Total Time: 15 minutes

Serves: 4

Calories: 334 kcal

Ingredients:

- 1 Lb. of ground beef
- 1 Taco seasoning pack
- ⅔ Cup of beef broth
- John Soules frozen beef steak strips
- 1 15 Oz. Jar of cheese dip
- Tortilla chips
- Mozzarella cheese

Cooking Instructions:

1. In a medium mixing bowl, merge together the beef, taco seasoning pack with beef broth, frozen beef steak strips. Stir thoroughly.
2. Put the mixture in the cooking tray. Lay the drip pan in the bottom of the cooking chamber.
3. Select the Air fry on the display panel. Set the temperature to 375°F and adjust the cooking time to 5 minutes.
4. Press the start. When the display panel show "Add Food", put the cooking tray in the center position.
5. When the unit show "turn food", ignore because the food is done. This goes with Tortilla chips. Top with mozzarella cheese.
6. Serve and enjoy!!!

Sticky Spicy Barbecue Wings

Preparation Time: 10 minutes

Cook Time: 20 minutes

Total Time: 30 minutes

Serves: 4

Calories: 197 kcal

Ingredients:

- 2 Lbs. Patty wings, seasoned with your favorite seasonings
- Honey, to taste
- Brown Sugar, to taste
- Barbecue Sauce
- Franks Red Hot sauce

Cooking Instructions:

1. In a large mixing bowl, put all the ingredients except the patty wings. Give it a nice stir. Put the wings in the cooking tray and pour the sauce over it. Stir well.
2. Lay the drip pan in the bottom of the cooking chamber. Select the Airfry on the display panel.
3. Set the temperature to 375°F and adjust the cooking time to 20 minutes.
4. Press the start. When the display panel show "Add Food", put the cooking tray in the center position.
5. When the unit show "turn food", ignore because the food is done.
6. Serve and enjoy!!!

Steak and Beef Nachos

Preparation Time: 10 minutes

Cook Time: 5 minutes

Total Time: 15 minutes

Serves: 4

Calories: 286 kcal

Ingredients:

- 1 Lb. of ground beef
- 1 Taco seasoning pack
- ⅔ Cup of beef broth
- John Soules frozen beef steak strips
- 1 15 Oz. jar of cheese dip
- Tortilla chips
- Mozzarella cheese

Cooking Instructions:

1. In a medium mixing bowl, merge together the beef, taco seasoning, beef broth, beef steak strips. Add the cheese dip. Place the mixture in the cooking tray.
2. Lay the drip pan in the bottom of the cooking chamber. Select the Airfry on the display panel.
3. Set the temperature to 370°F and adjust the cooking time to 5 minutes.
4. Press the start. When the display panel show "Add Food", put the cooking tray in the center position.
5. When the unit show "turn food", ignore because the food is done. Serve it over Tortilla chips and top with mozzarella cheese.
6. Serve and enjoy!!!

INSTANT VORTEX AIR FRYER DESSERT RECIPES

Grandmothers Pound Cake

Preparation Time: 10 minutes

Cook Time: 1 hour 50 minutes

Total Time: 2 hours

Serves: 4

Calories: 328 kcal

Ingredients:

- 1 Cup of Crisco
- 2 Cups of sugar
- 5 Eggs
- 2 Cups of flour
- ⅓ Cup of orange juice
- 1 Tsp. vanilla
- ½ Tsp. lemon extract
- ¼ Tsp. salt

Cooking Instructions:

1. Combine together the Crisco and sugar, put eggs 1 at a time and beat with your mixer between each one.
2. Add 1 cup of flour with orange juice and beat. Add second cup of flour and beat properly.
3. Put vanilla, lemon extract and salt. Place the mixture in the cooking tray.
4. Lay the drip pan in the bottom of the cooking chamber. Select the Airfry on the display panel.
5. Set the temperature to 370°F and adjust the cooking time to 1 hours 50 minutes.
6. Press the start. When the display panel show "Add Food", put the cooking tray in the center position.
7. When the unit show "turn food", ignore because the food is done. Serve it over Tortilla chips and top with mozzarella cheese.
8. Serve and enjoy!!!

Half a Cake

Preparation Time: 10 minutes

Cook Time: 35 minutes

Total Time: 45 minutes

Serves: 4

Calories: 228 kcal

Ingredients:

- 1¾ Cup of mix from 18 Oz. box of cake mix
- ⅔ Cup of liquid
- ¼ Cup of oil
- 1 Egg

Cooking Instructions:

1. Spray the cooking tray with nonstick baking spray containing flour and set aside. In medium bowl, merge together the cake mix, liquid, oil, and egg. Stir well.
2. Beat for 1 minute at medium speed. Pour the mixture into the cooking tray. Lay the drip pan in the bottom of the cooking chamber.
3. Select the Air fry on the display panel. Set the temperature to 370°F and adjust the cooking time to 35 minutes.
4. Press the start. When the display panel show "Add Food", put the cooking tray in the center position.
5. When the unit show "turn food", ignore because the food is done. Dust with powdered sugar.
6. Serve and enjoy!!!

Funfetti Cupcakes

Preparation Time: 10 minutes

Cook Time: 25 minutes

Total Time: 35 minutes

Serves: 4

Calories: 311 kcal

Ingredients:

- ⅔ Cup of water
- ⅛ Cup of oil
- 2 Egg whites
- 1 (8 Oz.) Funfetti Cupcake and Cake Mix

Cooking Instructions:

1. With a six cup muffin pan, place cupcake liners. In a large mixing bowl, merge together cake mix, water, oil, and egg whites. Give it a nice stir.
2. Put batter into each muffin cup filling about ⅔ full. Lay the drip pan in the bottom of the cooking chamber.
3. Select the Air fry on the display panel. Set the temperature to 360°F and adjust the cooking time to 25 minutes.
4. Press the start. When the display panel show "Add Food", put the muffin pan in the center position.
5. When the unit show "turn food", ignore because the food is done. Dust with powdered sugar.
6. Serve and enjoy!!!

Duncan Hines Red Velvet Cake

Preparation Time: 10 minutes

Cook Time: 60 minutes

Total Time: 1 hour 10 minutes

Serves: 4

Calories: 250 kcal

Ingredients:

- Red Velvet cake mix
- 1 Can of pumpkin
- ½ Tsp. pumpkin pie spice
- ½ Tsp. vanilla bean paste

Cooking Instructions:

1. In a medium mixing bowl, mix all the ingredients together and pour it into the cooking tray.
2. Lay the drip pan in the bottom of the cooking chamber. Select the Airfry on the display panel. Set the temperature to 360°F and adjust the cooking time to 1 hour.
3. Press the start. When the display panel show "Add Food", put the cooking tray in the center position.
4. When the unit show "turn food", ignore because the food is done. This goes with whipped cream.
5. Serve and enjoy!!!

Dump Cake-Apple Spice

Preparation Time: 10 minutes

Cook Time: 25 minutes

Total Time: 35 minutes

Serves: 2

Calories: 216 kcal

Ingredients:

- 2 (20 Oz.) Cans of Apple Pie Filling
- 1 Box of Spice cake mix
- 2 Sticks of butter

Cooking Instructions:

1. Put the pie filling in the cooking tray. Sprinkle the box of cake mix on top. Cut the butter and spread on top of cake mix.
2. Lay the drip pan in the bottom of the cooking chamber. Select the Airfry on the display panel.
3. Set the temperature to 360°F and adjust the cooking time to 25 minutes.
4. Press the start. When the display panel show "Add Food", put the cooking tray in the center position.
5. When the unit show "turn food", ignore because the food is done.
6. Serve and enjoy!!!

Dump Cake-Fresh Blueberries

Preparation Time: 10 minutes

Cook Time: 20 minutes

Total Time: 30 minutes

Serves: 2

Calories: 320 kcal

Ingredients:

- 3 Cups of fresh blueberries
- 1 Can of crushed pineapple, undrained
- ½ Cup of brown sugar sprinkled on top of fruit
- 1 Butter cake mix, dry crumbled on top of fruit
- 1 Stick of melted butter on top of cake mix
- Bluebell Homemade Vanilla

Cooking Instructions:

1. In a medium mixing bowl, mix all the ingredients together. Give it a nice stir. Place the mixture in the cooking tray.
2. Lay the drip pan in the bottom of the cooking chamber. Select the Airfry on the display panel.
3. Set the temperature to 360°F and adjust the cooking time to 20 minutes.
4. Press the start. When the display panel show "Add Food", put the cooking tray in the center position.
5. When the unit show "turn food", ignore because the food is done.
6. Serve and enjoy!!!

Divine Boxed Brownies

Preparation Time: 10 minutes

Cook Time: 20 minutes

Total Time: 30 minutes

Serves: 4

Calories: 178 kcal

Ingredients:

- 1 Box of brownie mix
- PAM
- 1 Cup of chocolate syrup
- 1 Cup of water
- Nuts
- Chocolate chips

Cooking Instructions:

1. Begin by mixing the boxed brownies and pour it into the cooking tray. Sprinkle on top of the brownie mixture, nuts and chocolate chips.
2. Mix together the chocolate syrup and water. Stir thoroughly and pour the syrup mixture on top of the nuts and chocolate chips.
3. Place the cups in the cooking tray. Lay the drip pan in the bottom of the cooking chamber.
4. Select the Air fry on the display panel. Select the temperature to 360°F and adjust the cooking time to 20 minutes.
5. Press the start. When the display panel show "Add Food", put the cooking tray in the center position.
6. When the unit show "turn food", ignore because the food is done.
7. Serve and enjoy!!!

Corn Pudding

Preparation Time: 10 minutes

Cook Time: 30 minutes

Total Time: 40 minutes

Serves: 4

Calories: 438 kcal

Ingredients:

- 2 Eggs
- 1 Tbsp. flour
- 2 Tbsp. sugar
- 1 14 Oz. can whole corn, drained
- 1 14 Oz. can creamed corn

Cooking Instructions:

1. In a medium mixing bowl, mix all the ingredients together. Give it a nice stir. Spray cooking tray with butter flavored cooking spray.
2. Place the mixture in the cooking tray. Lay the drip pan in the bottom of the cooking chamber.
3. Select the Air fry on the display panel. Set the temperature to 380°F and adjust the cooking time to 30 minutes.
4. Press the start. When the display panel show "Add Food", put the cooking tray in the center position.
5. When the unit show "turn food", ignore because the food is done.
6. Serve and enjoy!!!

Cranberry Banana Cake

Preparation Time: 10 minutes

Cook Time: 50 minutes

Total Time: 60 minutes

Serves: 3

Calories: 348 kcal

Ingredients:

- 1 Cake mix
- 5 Over ripe bananas, smashed
- ½ Cup of rehydrated cranberries

Cooking Instructions:

1. In a medium mixing bowl, mix all the ingredients together. Give it a nice stir. Place the mixture in the cooking tray.
2. Lay the drip pan in the bottom of the cooking chamber. Select the Airfry on the display panel.
3. Set the temperature to 370°F and adjust the cooking time to 50 minutes.
4. Press the start. When the display panel show "Add Food", put the cooking tray in the center position.
5. When the unit show "turn food", ignore because the food is done.
6. Serve and enjoy!!!

Christmas Nut Clusters

Preparation Time: 10 minutes

Cook Time: 35 minutes

Total Time: 45 minutes

Serves: 3

Calories: 286 kcal

Ingredients:

- 1 16 Oz. jar unsalted peanuts
- 1 16 Oz. jar salted peanuts
- 1 12 Oz. package semi-sweet chocolate chips
- 1 12 Oz. package milk chocolate chips
- 2 10 Oz. packages of peanut butter chips
- 2 1 Lb. packages of white almond bark

Cooking Instructions:

1. In a medium mixing bowl, mix all the ingredients together. Give it a nice stir. Place the mixture in the cooking tray.
2. Lay the drip pan in the bottom of the cooking chamber. Select the Airfry on the display panel.
3. Set the temperature to 370°F and adjust the cooking time to 35 minutes.
4. Press the start. When the display panel show "Add Food", put the cooking tray in the center position.
5. When the unit show "turn food", ignore because the food is done.
6. Serve and enjoy!!!

Cinnamon Caramel Apples

Preparation Time: 10 minutes

Cook Time: 20 minutes

Total Time: 30 minutes

Serves: 2

Calories: 318 kcal

Ingredients:

- 3 Apples, cut in two and seeds removed
- Cinnamon
- Sugar to taste
- Caramel
- Vanilla ice cream

Cooking Instructions:

1. Place all the ingredients in the cooking tray except vanilla ice cream and caramel. Give it a nice stir and drizzle caramel on the top.
2. Lay the drip pan in the bottom of the cooking chamber. Select the Airfry on the display panel.
3. Set the temperature to 370°F and adjust the cooking time to 20 minutes.
4. Press the start. When the display panel show "Add Food", put the cooking tray in the center position.
5. When the unit show "turn food", ignore because the food is done. Top with vanilla ice cream.
6. Serve and enjoy!!!

www.ingramcontent.com/pod-product-compliance
Lightning Source LLC
Chambersburg PA
CBHW081753100526
44592CB00015B/2410